ASSESSMENT

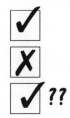 ??

ASSESSMENT

CASE STUDIES, EXPERIENCE AND
PRACTICE FROM HIGHER EDUCATION

EDITED BY
PETER SCHWARTZ AND GRAHAM WEBB

CASE STUDIES OF TEACHING IN HIGHER EDUCATION

**KOGAN
PAGE**

First published in 2002

Kogan Page Limited
120 Pentonville Road
London N1 9JN
UK

Stylus Publishing Inc.
22883 Quicksilver Drive
Sterling VA 20166-2012
USA

British Library Cataloguing in Publication Data

A CIP record for this book is available from the British Library.

ISBN 0 7494 3623 9 (paperback)
ISBN 0 7494 3689 1 (hardback)

Typeset by Saxon Graphics Ltd, Derby
Printed and bound in Great Britain by Biddles Ltd, Guildford and King's Lynn
www.biddles.co.uk

Contents

Section 5: Addressing the Needs of Individual Students in Assessment

Section 6: Hands-on Assessment: Everyday Problems in Assessment Practice

Contributors

Adina Bailey is Test Coordinator, Center for Assessment and Research Studies, James Madison University, Harrisonburg, VA, USA (e-mail: assessment@jmu.edu).

Trudy W Banta is Professor of Higher Education and Vice Chancellor for Planning and Institutional Improvement at Indiana University–Purdue University Indianapolis, IN, USA (e-mail: tbanta@iupui.edu).

David Baume is Director of Teaching Development in the Centre for Higher Education Practice, The Open University, Milton Keynes, UK (e-mail: a.d.baume@open.ac.uk).

Kenneth W Borland, Jr was, at the time of writing, Assistant Vice Provost for Academic Affairs and Director of Assessment at Montana State University, Bozeman, MT, USA. He is now Associate Provost at East Stroudsburg University, East Stroudsburg, PA, USA (e-mail: kborland@po-box.esu.edu).

Carol Bowie is Lecturer in the Griffith Institute for Higher Education, Griffith University, Brisbane, Australia (e-mail: c.bowie@mailbox.gu.edu.au).

Sally Brown is Director of Membership Services at the UK's Institute for Learning and Teaching and is Visiting Professor at the Robert Gordon University, Aberdeen, Scotland (e-mail: sally.brown@ilt.ac.uk).

Chris H J Davies is a Senior Lecturer in the School of Physics and Materials Engineering at Monash University, Melbourne, Australia (e-mail: Chris.Davies@spme.monash.edu.au).

Louise F Deretchin is Director of Higher Education for The Houston Annenberg Challenge, Houston, TX, USA and Adjunct Professor at the University of St Thomas and Baylor College of Medicine. At the time of writing, she was Education Director, Academic Informatics Services at Baylor College of Medicine, Houston, TX, USA (e-mail: lderetchin@houston.rr.com).

Melissa de Zwart is a Lecturer in the Law Faculty at Monash University, Melbourne, Australia (e-mail: melissa.dezwart@law.monash.edu.au).

T Dary Erwin is Director, Center for Assessment and Research Studies, and Professor of Psychology at James Madison University, Harrisonburg, VA, USA (e-mail: erwintd@jmu.edu).

Nancy Falchikov was, until recently, Senior Lecturer in Psychology at Napier University, Edinburgh, UK. She now works in Educational Development Services at Napier and is a Research Fellow in the Department of Higher and Further Education at the University of Edinburgh (e-mail: n.falchikov@napier.ac.uk).

Peter Grebenik is in the School of Biological and Molecular Sciences at Oxford Brookes University, UK (e-mail: pgrebenik@brookes.ac.uk).

Sharon J Hamilton is a Chancellor's Professor in the Department of English and Director of the Faculty Colloquium for Excellence in Teaching at Indiana University–Purdue University Indianapolis, IN, USA (e-mail: shamilton@iupui.edu).

Susan Hodgson is Senior Lecturer in the division of Childhood and Family Studies at the University of Northumbria at Newcastle, UK (e-mail: susan.hodgson@unn.ac.uk).

Gordon Joughin was at the time of writing an Educational Designer in Griffith Flexible Learning Services, Griffith University, Brisbane, Australia. He is currently Coordinator, Teaching and Learning Services at the Queensland Police Services Academy, Australia (e-mail: gjoughin@optushome.com.au).

Di Marks-Maran is Head of the School of Research and Postgraduate Studies at Thames Valley University, London, UK (e-mail: di.marks-maran@tvu.ac.uk).

Liz McDowell is Networked Learning Project Manager at the University of Northumbria, Newcastle upon Tyne, UK (e-mail: liz.mcdowell@unn.ac.uk).

Keith Miller is a Senior Lecturer in the School of Education at the University of Northumbria, Newcastle upon Tyne, UK (e-mail: keith.miller@unn.ac.uk).

Sue Miller is Senior Lecturer and Course Leader for Care & Education of Very Young Children in the division of Childhood and Family Studies at the University of Northumbria at Newcastle upon Tyne, UK (e-mail: sue.miller@unn.ac.uk).

Phil Race is an independent consultant in higher education in the UK and beyond (e-mail: Phil@Phil-Race.net) (Web site: www.Phil-Race.net).

Tim Riordan is Associate Dean for Academic Affairs and Professor of Philosophy at Alverno College in Milwaukee, WI, USA (e-mail: tim.riordan@alverno.edu).

Chris Rust is Head of the Oxford Centre for Staff and Learning Development and Deputy Director of the Human Resource Directorate at Oxford Brookes University, UK (e-mail: cirust@brookes.ac.uk).

D Royce Sadler is Professor of Higher Education at Griffith University, Brisbane, Australia (e-mail: r.sadler@mailbox.gu.edu.au).

Kay Sambell is Senior Lecturer and Course Leader for Childhood Studies in the division of Childhood and Family Studies at the University of Northumbria at Newcastle upon Tyne, UK (e-mail: kay.sambell@unn.ac.uk).

Peter Schwartz is Associate Professor in Pathology at the University of Otago Medical School, Dunedin, New Zealand (e-mail: peter.schwartz@stonebow.otago.ac.nz).

Lorraine Stefani is a Reader in the Centre for Academic Practice, University of Strathclyde, Glasgow, UK (e-mail: l.stefani@strath.ac.uk).

Keith Sullivan is a Senior Lecturer in the School of Education at Victoria University of Wellington, New Zealand (e-mail: keith.sullivan@vuw.ac.nz).

Peter Taylor is Senior Lecturer in the Griffith Institute for Higher Education, Griffith University, Brisbane, Australia (e-mail: peter.taylor@mailbox.gu.edu.au).

Graham Webb is Professor and Director, Centre for Higher Education Quality at Monash University, Melbourne, VIC, Australia (e-mail: Graham.Webb@adm.monash.edu.au).

Helen Woodward is Senior Lecturer and Course Coordinator for the Primary Education Program in the College of Arts, Education and Social Sciences at the University of Western Sydney, Australia (e-mail: h.woodward@uws.edu.au).

Barbara D Wright is Associate Professor of German at the University of Connecticut, Storrs, CT, USA (e-mail: barbara.wright@uconn.edu).

Mantz Yorke is Professor of Higher Education at Liverpool John Moores University, UK (e-mail: m.yorke@livjm.ac.uk).

Brad Young is an Educational Designer in Griffith Flexible Learning Services, Griffith University, Brisbane, Australia (e-mail: b.young@mailbox. gu.edu.au).

Gill Young is Reader in Educational Development at Thames Valley University, London, UK (e-mail: gill.young@tvu.ac.uk).

Craig Zimitat is Lecturer in the Griffith Institute for Higher Education, Griffith University, Brisbane, Australia (e-mail: c.zimitat@mailbox.gu.edu.au).

INTRODUCTION

Two things are certain. First, there is unparalleled change in higher education. Far more students are studying at universities and other institutions of higher education than ever before. They come from a wider cross-section of society and are studying in many and varied ways. For example, many are now classed as 'mature' students who fit their studies in around their normal jobs. Even those who go straight on to higher education from school routinely obtain part-time employment while attending classes so that they can pay for their education. And 'attending classes' has become a variable phenomenon, as face-to-face teaching is augmented and, in some cases, replaced by online discussion groups and a wide range of multimedia learning resources.

Second, everyone knows that assessment is the main 'driver' of learning. We know this from the past 30 years and more of educational research. We know that despite pleas for students to 'read widely' or undertake all kinds of educationally engaging activity, they quickly distinguish rhetoric from reality and direct their activities to the reality of what is required in terms of assessment. The normal behaviour of both individuals and organizations is to gear their activities and behaviour towards satisfying the requirements of assessment. This means that assessment needs to provide a transparent and meaningful link between learning activities and desired learning outcomes as the very nature of the learning undertaken can be subverted by an inappropriate assessment regime.

So, at a time of unparalleled change, and with assessment being of such importance for both moulding and assuring the nature of learning undertaken, it is no surprise to find that assessment has received extensive coverage in the literature. Why then bother to produce yet another book on assessment?

What makes this book different is that it takes the reader right into the middle of 'real-life' situations that have actually occurred as teachers grapple with important current issues concerning assessment. It draws upon the actual experiences of teachers from a number of countries, over a range of disciplinary areas and facing a variety of assessment problems. Having said that, considerable care has been taken to ensure that a reader from any disciplinary background or area will find each case of interest.

This introduction provides a brief discussion of assessment – what it is and how it is used – together with some pointers to issues in the theory and practice of assessment in higher education. It is intended as a starting point rather than a comprehensive review. The nature of the cases is then introduced followed by some suggestions on how to use the book in order to get the most out of it.

WHAT IS ASSESSMENT?

If the origin of the word 'assessment' is somewhat obscure (Freeman and Lewis, 1998), so, too, is its usage today. Rowntree (1987) and Freeman and Lewis (1998) identify a number of purposes of assessment, including: selection; certification/accreditation; maintenance of standards; description (eg in the form of a profile); motivation; improving learning; and improving teaching. Indeed, it can be observed that the purpose ascribed to assessment varies with the purpose ascribed to the entire project of higher education (see, for example, Bowden and Marton, 1998; Brown and Glasner, 1999; Miller, Imrie and Cox, 1998).

That having been said, two distinct interpretations of 'assessment' became apparent as we developed this book. Firstly, in the United Kingdom and Australasia, assessment is interpreted in terms of the routine tasks that students undertake in order to receive feedback on their learning and a mark or grade signifying their achievement. In the United States on the other hand, assessment has recently been applied to processes at the institutional level. Cases focusing on institutional-level assessment have been grouped together in Section Three, while cases that have a more direct teacher–student–classroom context feature in all other sections. Throughout the book the emphasis is on the assessment of student learning, rather than on attempts to evaluate teachers or teaching.

ISSUES IN ASSESSMENT

The literature on assessment is voluminous. Apart from the sources already cited, there are many guides and handbooks to help the teacher in higher education navigate towards a sensible assessment strategy and use of appropriate assessment vehicles (eg Angelo and Cross, 1993; Crooks, 1988a; George and Cowan, 1999; Habeshaw, Gibbs and Habeshaw, 1993). There are examples of assessment in practice (eg Nightingale *et al*, 1996) and examples of assessment in a variety of teaching contexts (eg Jaques (2000) in terms of group learning; Boud (1995) in terms of self-assessment).

Perhaps the most consistent message to come from this literature (see for example Crooks, 1988b) is the importance of selecting an appropriate assessment strategy to support the major objectives of the curriculum.

> Student learning research has repeatedly demonstrated the impact of assessment on students' approaches to learning.... Ask them to understand the physics and chemistry of muscle contraction, but test them on the names of the muscles, and they will 'learn' the names but not be able to explain how contraction happens. Ask students to understand narrative perspective in the novel but test them on the author's background and they will know a lot about the author and little about narrative perspective.
>
> (Nightingale and O'Neil, 1994, pp 149–50)

Identifying the major objectives of the curriculum has seen progression from testing conceptual or disciplinary knowledge, to testing the application of that knowledge in different contexts, together with a wider appreciation of or sensitivity to the boundaries and changing nature of knowledge. And not only is disciplinary knowledge now developed and tested in more flexible and contingent ways, but the *general* skills and abilities of students are increasingly developed and tested within disciplinary contexts. Lifelong learning skills have become an important and explicit feature of the curriculum (Candy, Crebert and O'Leary, 1994) and the call for evidence of 'graduate', 'transferable' or 'generic' skills and attributes in students (eg oral and written communication, teamwork, self-management, creativity, inquiry and problem solving etc) places new demands on assessment.

The need to demonstrate understanding and application of knowledge, together with generic skills, has moved assessment practice towards new vehicles. It is clear that while a handwritten, three-hour, essay-type examination may be able to legitimately test some things, it cannot test all, especially the generic skills that students have developed. This has led to 'integrated' or 'authentic' assessment becoming more important. In such assessment, 'complex simulations, case studies, role plays or multi-faceted projects . . . are used to assess a range of knowledge, skills and attitudes in the one assessment' (Nightingale *et al*, 1996, p 3). And in situations where self-reflection is important (are there any where it is not?), reflective journals or reflective moments in portfolios have become popular. In short, testing what students can actually do, and their own appreciation of how they have developed and need to continue to develop their learning, marks a significant shift in approach to assessment.

At the same time, higher education practice is notoriously slow to change and surprisingly resilient in the face of the body of higher education theory and practice that has developed over the past 30 years or so. While there may be legitimate concerns about the integrity of new assessment vehicles – sometimes centred on increasing opportunities for cheating, plagiarism and dishonesty on the part of students, or problems with marking reliability or bias on the part of examiners – there is also considerable resistance born of inertia, conservatism and a lack of professionalization in terms of teaching qualification, induction and continuing professional development.

Assessment poses a number of tensions, including that between the 'validity' and 'reliability' of assessment processes. Validity means that an assessment actually measures what it is supposed to measure and, one hopes, that this is something important and meaningful. On the other hand, reliability refers to the consistency of measurement – that repeat measures (including by other people) will lead to a similar or identical result. Not surprisingly, the greater the attempt to control an assessment task in order to ensure reliable measurement, the greater is the temptation to diminish its 'reality', meaning or validity. The question often comes down to where we wish to draw the line between accurate measurement of the trivial, and unstable measurement of the important.

There are two other perennial 'tensions' in the theory and practice of assessment in higher education. The perceived need to judge the performance of students relative to each other (in order to award scholarships, for example) leads to norm-referenced assessment, which was the dominant form of assessment in many universities. On the other hand, if student performance is to be judged against established standards (referred to as criterion-referenced assessment), the criteria for achievement must be carefully developed and explained to students, and their performance is then gauged relative to these criteria, rather than relative to each other. In fact, however, there tend to be features of both norm- and criterion-based practice in most assessment tasks. There is also tension between grading student work for the purpose of demonstrating attainment of a standard (summative assessment) and giving students feedback on their work so that they may improve (formative assessment). Again, much assessment practice includes elements of both, but it is probably true to say that there has tended to be greater emphasis on summative than on formative assessment. In general, modern assessment practice appears to be moving towards criterion-based assessment and towards acknowledgement of the importance of formative assessment in helping students learn and improve.

This then is the territory of assessment in higher education and the context within which, as teachers in higher education, we attempt to assess our students. It is the territory within which the cases that are reported in this book have developed. We now turn to those cases before offering some guidance on how the cases might most profitably be approached.

THE CASES

The cases in this book follow the format of others in the series (Edwards, Smith and Webb, 2001; Murphy, Walker and Webb, 2001; Schwartz, Mennin and Webb, 2001). In fact, there are rich interconnections and insights to be gained from considering assessment alongside issues explored in those volumes, which deal with lecturing, online teaching and learning, and problem-based learning, respectively.

The 22 cases have been developed by 34 faculty members from Australia, New Zealand, the United Kingdom and the United States. They come from a wide range of disciplines and areas as diverse as education, law, medicine, engineering, biological and molecular sciences, educational development and philosophy. Each case tells the story of an actual incident that took place and that was of some considerable importance to the teacher. These are real stories and the authenticity of the experience is evident in each of the cases.

As with all books in this series, each case is preceded by an indication of the main issue or issues raised and by brief background information to set the context for the 'action'. The case proper consists of two or more parts, each part concluding with a few questions to consider. This reflective break always occurs at a point where an action must be taken and/or a decision made. At this point, you are invited to step into the writer's shoes and decide not only what you think *should* be done next but also what you think *will actually happen* next, given the circumstances of the case. Then, after discovering what actually *did* happen, you are asked to reflect on how the situation was handled and to consider some of the questions and issues raised by the case. At the end there is a case reporter's discussion that raises questions such as the following:

- How well was the situation handled?
- What other options might there have been for dealing with it?
- What lessons did the reporter and his or her colleagues learn from the experience?
- What lessons are there for you from the case?

The discussions are by no means exhaustive and you may well identify other issues or perspectives that have not been mentioned. We have tried to strike a balance between leaving each situation open to individual interpretation on the one hand, and tightly defining issues and providing guidance on the other. Nor is the discussion intended to give 'the right answer' to a problem. We do not believe that there is necessarily a simple and unequivocal 'right answer' in cases such as these, although given the circumstances described, some solutions may be better than others. The purpose of the discussion is to explore the issues raised and to encourage you to make your own decisions based upon your interpretation of and reflections on the case.

The issues brought out by the cases arose as a result of our suggestions to case writers of possible fertile areas for development and the input of case writers suggesting other interesting areas or issues. This resulted in the grouping of cases around the following themes or issues:

- information technology and assessment: especially concerning the use of computers to assist assessment in large classes (cases reported by Erwin and Bailey, Grebenik and Rust, Schwartz, and Brown);
- reflective assessment: journals, logbooks, portfolios and peer assessment (cases reported by Stefani, Woodward, Bowie *et al*, Baume and Yorke, and Falchikov);
- institution-wide assessment: especially the perspective brought by case writers from the United States (cases reported by Wright, Banta and Hamilton, and Borland);
- assessment methods for special purposes: particularly problem-based learning and short, intensive courses (cases reported by Young and Marks-Maran, Deretchin, and Sullivan);
- individual students and assessment: helping and relating to individual students in the context of assessment (cases reported by Sadler, Sambell *et al*, and Riordan);
- hands-on assessment: everyday problems in assessment practice (cases reported by Davies, Race, Miller and McDowell, and de Zwart).

HOW TO USE THIS BOOK

We strongly recommend that, as you read a case, you 'play the game' and read only Part One, before reflecting and noting your impressions of what is going on, what courses of action could be taken next, what you think *will* happen next and what course of action *you* would pursue. The same applies to Part Two (and others, where relevant). Questions have been provided at the end of each part of a case to assist you in framing your interpretation of and response to what is happening. As well as questions that are specific to the case, the following general questions are appropriate for most cases.

At the end of Part One, ask:

- What is going on here?
- What factors may have contributed to the situation described?
- How does the case reporter appear to see the situation?
- What *other* interpretations might there be?
- How might the situation be handled?
- What sorts of consequences might be expected from the possible actions?

- Given the nature of the participants, how will the situation probably be dealt with?

After the final part and the discussion, ask:

- How well was the situation handled?
- What general issues are brought out by the case?
- What do the case and its issues mean for you, the reader?

We believe that you will derive valuable insights if you use the case studies and discussions in this way. However, we suggest that you will also find it valuable to meet with colleagues to share impressions of the cases and insights obtained from them. The cases can serve as resources for advanced training and development. In fact, the cases presented in a previous book (Schwartz and Webb, 1993) were both the products of and the discussion materials for a series of group discussions in a faculty development programme. Others have also described the use of case studies in faculty development for teachers (Christensen, 1987; Hutchings, 1993; Wilkerson and Boehrer, 1992).

The book concludes with a list of further readings on assessment. Most of the readings are of general applicability rather than being directed toward specific issues or events discussed in the cases. The reading list is intended to be broad and immediately useful rather than comprehensive. The editors and contributors also welcome enquiries from readers who would like more information or dialogue, and electronic mail addresses are given for the editors and for case reporters.

We trust that reflection on assessment and on the issues raised by the cases presented in this book will be useful, and will stimulate you to try new approaches in your own teaching and assessment methods in order to enhance student learning. We wish you every success.

References

Angelo, T A and Cross, K P (1993) *Classroom Assessment Techniques: A handbook for college teachers* (2nd edn), Jossey-Bass, San Francisco, CA

Boud, D (1995) *Enhancing Learning through Self Assessment*, Kogan Page, London

Bowden, J and Marton, F (1998) *The University of Learning: Beyond quality and competence in higher education*, Kogan Page, London

Brown, S and Glasner, A (eds) (1999) *Assessment Matters in Higher Education: Choosing and using diverse approaches*, Society for Research into Higher Education & Open University Press, Buckingham, UK

Candy, P, Crebert, G and O'Leary, J (1994) *Developing Life Long Learning through Undergraduate Education*, commissioned report Number 28: NBEET, Government Publishing Service DEET, Canberra, Australia

Christensen, C R (1987) *Teaching and the Case Method*, Harvard Business School, Boston, MA

Crooks, T J (1988a) *Assessing Student Performance*, Green Guide No. 8, Higher Education Research and Development Society of Australasia, Kensington, NSW, Australia

Crooks, T J (1988b) 'The impact of classroom evaluation practices on students', *Review of Educational Research*, **58**, pp 438–81

Edwards, H, Smith, B and Webb, G (eds) (2001) *Lecturing: Case studies, experience and practice*, Kogan Page, London

Freeman, R and Lewis, R (1998) *Planning and Implementing Assessment*, Kogan Page, London

George, J and Cowan, J (1999) *A Handbook of Techniques for Formative Evaluation: Mapping the student's learning experience*, Kogan Page, London

Habeshaw, S, Gibbs, G and Habeshaw T (1993) *53 Interesting Ways to Assess Your Students* (3rd edn), Technical and Educational Services Ltd, Bristol, UK

Hutchings, P (1993) *Using Cases to Improve College Teaching: A guide to more reflective practice*, American Association for Higher Education, Washington, DC

Jaques, D (2000) *Learning in Groups* (3rd edn), Kogan Page, London

Miller, A H, Imrie, B W and Cox, K (1998) *Student Assessment in Higher Education: A handbook for assessing performance*, Kogan Page, London

Murphy, D, Walker, R and Webb, G (eds) (2001) *Online Learning & Teaching with Technology: Case studies, experience and practice*, Kogan Page, London

Nightingale, P and O'Neil, M (1994) *Achieving Quality Learning in Higher Education*, Kogan Page, London

Nightingale, P, Te Wiata, I, Toohey, S, Ryan, G, Hughes, C and Magin, D (1996) *Assessing Learning in Universities*, University of New South Wales Press, Sydney, Australia

Rowntree, D (1987) *Assessing Students: How shall we know them?* (rev edn), Kogan Page, London

Schwartz, P, Mennin, S and Webb, G (eds) (2001) *Problem-Based Learning: Case studies, experience and practice*, Kogan Page, London

Schwartz, P and Webb, G (1993) *Case Studies on Teaching in Higher Education*, Kogan Page, London

Wilkerson, L and Boehrer, J (1992) 'Using cases about teaching for faculty development', *To Improve the Academy*, **11**, pp 253–62

SECTION 1

INFORMATION TECHNOLOGY: ONE ANSWER TO ASSESSMENT IN LARGE CLASSES

CHAPTER 1

TAKING THE BYTE OUT OF COMPUTER-BASED TESTING

Case reporters: T Dary Erwin and Adina Bailey

Issues raised

This case raises the issue of managing some of the difficulties that arise when computer-based tests replace paper and pencil tests for campus-wide assessment.

Background

The Center for Assessment and Research Studies (CARS) at James Madison University (JMU) in Harrisonburg, Virginia, collaborated with the Office of Information Technology (OIT) and the General Education programme to open two computer-testing laboratories in 1999. During the 1999–2000 academic year, General Education Cluster 1, Skills for the 21st Century, required incoming first-year students to show competency in Microsoft Word, Microsoft PowerPoint, technology knowledge and information seeking by the end of their second semester. A 50-seat computer-testing lab was open approximately 25 hours per week for drop-in testing. Over 3,000 first-year students eventually completed their Cluster 1 competency tests during that first year of testing. The events described in this case took place during the first semester of that year and the first author is the narrator.

PART 1

This did not look promising! As I walked up the stairs, I began to see the students. There were at least 200 of them – maybe more – forming a staggered line down the hall. Some were sitting down and others were standing. I saw students eating their lunches and chatting with friends, while others were leaning against the wall with their eyes closed. These students had been waiting quite a while and, by the looks of things, they would probably be waiting some time yet.

I made my way down the hall to the entrance of the computer-testing lab. As I entered the lab, I saw Frank (one of the test proctors) leaning over a student's chair assisting with a login procedure, while our programmer/ analyst, David, was working on some kind of technical malfunction at an empty computer station. After a moment, I caught Frank's eye. He must have been surprised to see me, because he asked, 'Is everything okay?' I said, 'The proctor scheduled for this afternoon's session has cancelled and I'll be filling in for the rest of the day.' Frank raised an eyebrow and said wryly, 'What a convenient time for the proctor to have to cancel. I hope you're ready for a challenging afternoon!'

The lab was busier than it had been at any time during the semester so far. In August, I had accepted responsibility for staffing and scheduling the new computer-testing lab. For many weeks, the proctors had reported that only one or two students per week came to take the required tests. Had we recalled our own days as university students, we could probably have predicted that many students would procrastinate as long as possible before meeting their testing requirement. We were now at the day before the deadline and it was going to be a long afternoon.

The room was filled with 48 students because two of the available computers had crashed and would not reboot. Unfortunately, no one from computing support had been able to attend to the problem yet. I saw a girl over in the corner with her hand raised, so I asked her what was wrong. She said with feeling, 'I've just spent 20 minutes taking my PowerPoint test, but the computer froze while calculating my score. Now what happens?' I had seen this problem a few times during the semester, so I knew a few things to try. Unfortunately, all my efforts failed, so I had to tell her, 'I'm sorry, but you'll have to retake the test'. This particular student turned out to be more understanding than most, but I still found it difficult to have to tell her that her score was not retrievable.

As I moved on to the next request, I noticed that Frank and David, like me, were still busy assisting students with problems and questions. This time, a student told me, 'This test question says to underline the word "managed" in this sentence, but how can I do that when the word isn't there to underline?' This problem was easily solved, but now the student had less time to complete the rest of the timed exam. Throughout the semester, I had become aware that the software being used to assess competency in Microsoft Word and PowerPoint had some programming glitches, but the full consequences of these difficulties were only now becoming apparent as the volume of testing increased dramatically.

As I continued to walk around the room, I noticed that our Web-based, Information Seeking Skills Test (ISST) was particularly slow this day. Because this test is Web based, the items load most slowly at times when the network is getting the most use on campus. The ISST links students to specific databases where they can search for answers to test questions. Unfortunately, if the databases are unavailable for some reason, the student receives a 'failure to connect' message and cannot respond to the question. One frustrated student asked, 'How in the world am I supposed to meet the testing deadline when I can't even get the test to work?!'

So went the 'long afternoon'. I wish I could say that my experience in the testing lab that afternoon was unique – but I can't and it wasn't. As each testing deadline came and passed during that first semester, the experience was repeated. The more time I spent in the lab, the more I wished we could go back to using the faithful paper tests, pencils and bubble answer sheets. As long as I had enough supplies for everyone, the tests always 'worked'. Ah for the 'good old days'. Realistically, I knew that we had to forge ahead with our computer-testing efforts, but I also knew that we had to do something about the problems – and quickly. What were the most important issues to deal with? And what should we do?

What steps would you recommend taking to improve the performance of the computer-testing programme?
What do you think was actually done?

PART 2

Well, we did not make it through our first semester of computer-based testing as gracefully as I had hoped, but we did make it through. The majority of students had completed their required tests by the end of the semester and we had a readable data file for each test. Based on our experiences with implementing computer-based testing on such a large scale, we identified a number of crucial issues and began revising the testing process immediately. Our two primary groups of concerns were technical and administrative and they led to the following conclusions:

- The testing software had to be properly evaluated and made more reliable.

- The dependability of the Web-based parts of the test had to be improved.
- The scheduling of testing had to be improved so that overcrowding would not occur at particular times.
- Overall management of the testing lab had to be more clearly defined.

After our first semester's experience in the lab, we realized that there were several problems with the software that was assessing the students' knowledge of Microsoft Word and PowerPoint. First, the software interface was not user-friendly. As a result, two pages of written directions were needed to assist students to begin their tests. In addition to the difficulty of getting logged in to take the exam in the first place, students were often being kicked out of the test because of various programming errors. At one point, we calculated an error rate of 6 per cent for our testing sessions. Basically, 3 out of every 50 students were being forced to retake a test because of the inconsistency of the testing software.

This error rate concerned us, and we shared this information with others in our Assessment Center. We decided that an error rate above 1 per cent was unacceptable, and we requested a meeting with all the relevant parties at JMU and the software company. Frank, David and I along with other members from our respective offices and representatives from OIT attended a meeting early in the second semester. At this meeting, we learnt that JMU was the first institution to implement this software for such widespread testing. We were discovering problems that no one else had ever seen. The software company representative agreed that the company would address these problems in a new version of the software that would be released in a few months.

Before agreeing to use the software again, however, our Center's director requested a mass pilot testing of the new software before use the following academic year (2000–01). When we attended the pilot testing in August, we found that the software company had made noticeable improvements in the interface and having almost 40 people enter the software simultaneously did not crash the system. We began using the new software in September 2000. Along with the many improvements over the previous year, a few new problems cropped up as well. (For example, on the PowerPoint test, students were instructed to move a slide to the end of the presentation. When they performed the task, they received an error message: 'An error has occurred and this exam will be shut down'. Beneath that window could be seen the PowerPoint window error that 'This program has performed an illegal operation and will be shut down'. Since it was proprietary testing software, there was little we could do about the problem.) Overall, the software had been improved from the previous year, but evaluating its weaknesses and bringing them to the attention of the software company will be an ongoing process.

Just as the software we purchased presented challenges, the Web-based tests developed by CARS presented another technical problem. As a result of being Web based, these tests were slow at those times when the network was busy or bogged down. The movement of student response data between the computer lab and the file server was often delayed. This was not a problem for tests in which all the items were loaded at once and the student merely scrolled down through the test, but, unfortunately, a slow exchange between the lab computer and the server limited severely the possibility of implementing computer-adaptive tests. On such tests, a student is given his or her next test item based on the response to a previous item. This back-and-forth interaction between lab computers and the server was found to be painfully slow during peak times. We are in the process of trying a variety of possible solutions. First, we are looking at the physical location of the file server. Although we have fibre optic cable, having responses travel long distances and through routers might slow transmissions. Second, when we cannot move a file server to the respective computer-testing lab, we are trying to reduce the numbers of routers and nodes that transmitted responses have to pass. Third, we are looking at how responses are transferred, one test item at a time or the entire test transmitted as a whole.

One of our administrative concerns was the long line of students that formed around testing deadlines, resulting in students having to wait two hours or more to take their tests. Typically, students were not particularly excited about required testing anyway, so the long wait made their experience less pleasant. During the first year of testing, we had only one 50-seat computer lab available. Initially, we had made drop-in testing available all semester long, but we found that most students waited until a day or two before the deadline to come to take their tests.

Our second year of computer-based testing commenced at the start of the 2000–01 academic year, and part of our solution to the problem of over-crowding has been to open an additional 100-seat computer lab. We have also developed a system of staggered testing deadlines, based on students' ID numbers. At JMU, student ID numbers are randomly assigned. Our 3,000 first-year students have been divided into groups of approximately 300 by assigning testing deadlines based on the last digit of their ID numbers. Groups of about 300 students will match our current testing resources, because we now have computer lab seating for 150 students. By having the students in smaller groups, we have been able to set 10 different testing deadlines, whereby we can accommodate all of the students who will be attending.

Typically, the testing lab is not open for many evening hours during the semester because it is difficult to staff the lab, and most students have time during the day when they can come in for testing. On days that coincide with deadlines, the test administrator schedules evening lab hours to minimize problems for students who have schedule conflicts. Another approach we have incorporated to help reduce waiting lines is that faculty members have been encouraged to schedule times near the beginning of the semester when they could bring their classes by for testing.

A further administrative concern that we had about the testing lab during its first year was its management – a responsibility that was mine that year. Trying to manage the lab part-time was difficult as the demand for its use increased. The first year, we staffed the lab with graduate students who were trained to be proctors. Piecing together a schedule that would provide good coverage and evening hours was difficult. I also found it difficult to inform eight different proctors about the solution to a specific problem or about a policy change. Because of the location of my office, there were many times that I could not be at the lab, and I thought to myself that it would be better to be closer when difficulties arose. Eventually, a lab manager was hired to coordinate proctors and work with the different parties on campus who were involved in the computer-based testing effort.

Implementing computer-based testing has been a challenge that will continue. As our tests and technology continue to evolve, there will be new issues to address and old issues to be reconsidered. However, we believe that working through the challenges posed by computer-based testing has definitely been worth the effort.

How well do you think the problems were handled?
What alternatives might there have been?
What general lessons can be drawn from the case?

CASE REPORTERS' DISCUSSION

We learnt many lessons when the transition from paper/pencil testing to computer-based testing occurred. First, when a computer-testing lab is being established, it is important to consider how the network will be set up and where the servers will be located. We described in the case how these factors affected our computer-testing programme.

Other technical issues involve software and hardware. Regarding software, will the Internet be used in a Web-based test or will a microcomputer-based test be constructed? If a Web-based test is chosen, occasions when the Internet response time is slow must be expected. With some tests, selected Web sites and pages can be copied and the test made to look as though one is going 'to the Web'. We have had trouble using PERL code and now use JavaScript. And although the Web was originally created for text (ie HTML) exchanges, improvements are on the way.

Also with respect to software, before settling on the purchase or lease of any proprietary testing software, it is wise to check out the helpfulness of the company's support personnel. When we could identify particular problems in the software, we had difficulty getting the software company to correct the mistakes. If they say a correction will be included in the next version, it would pay to find out when the next version will be available.

Regarding hardware, what level of microcomputer is being considered for purchase? Strictly speaking, Web-based tests may not need large memory. If a test requires more calculations or distributed processing, the microcomputer must have sufficient memory and processing speed. We recommend head-phones so that audio capabilities may be exploited. For instance, in our oral communication test, students listened to speeches and small group discus-sions. Video capacity of the microcomputer is a consideration when students view art or other visual images.

At the same time, when multimedia capabilities are utilized in a testing situation, network personnel should be contacted to determine how best, or if, such media can be transported. We had good cooperation with network personnel in piloting the simultaneous transmission of a test response over the network. We had software work beautifully with 25 people, but the same software failed when over 50 students were attempting the same computer test.

Lastly, since so much can go wrong, we recommend being prepared for other problems to crop up.

Since technical problems are certain to arise, it is a distinct advantage to have an employee who can spend time addressing the technical and mana-gerial side of the lab. This individual can keep the lab staffed, correct minor technical problems and collaborate with the different departments on campus that are involved with the testing. The lab manager can also be involved with providing feedback to the software company or the individuals on campus who have developed a computer-based test. Having a structure in place that facilitates communication between the many different groups who are involved is helpful.

Another lesson we learnt is the importance of doing sufficient pilot testing. One person working with the software is not enough. If a lab seats 20 people, have 20 people take the test at once. If a lab seats 120 people, have 120 people take the test at once. In our experience, as volume increased, different problems often arose. Most importantly, try to crash the test. Students are going to have different levels of computer knowledge, and they may not take the test exactly as directed. Simulate the mistakes that students could make and see how the test responds. If a test is Web based, test it out during different times of the day. Things may look fine in the morning, but problems could arise in the afternoon when the network is busy. Having staff from an Office of Information Technology on call during peak testing times can also be helpful.

When computer-based testing is begun, it is wise to have a back-up plan. On a certain day, at a certain time, things might not go as expected, but students still need to be able to complete their tests. Having a PC version or an analogous paper and pencil test are possible back-up steps.

Despite its difficulties, computer-based testing has great potential benefits:

- Students can get immediate feedback.
- New test question formats can be explored (multimedia, art, graphics, sound).
- Word processed essays may be rated quickly with new software.

For large-scale testing of the sort introduced by JMU, computer-based testing offers advantages of efficiency, cost-effectiveness and convenience that are unlikely to be matched by any other form of testing currently available.

CHAPTER 2

IT TO THE RESCUE

Case reporters: Peter Grebenik and Chris Rust

Issues raised

This case focuses on the issues of assessing a large class, encouraging and supporting students who lack confidence or interest in a subject, and giving students formative feedback on their progress.

Background

The case study involves an Introductory Chemistry module in a UK university. It is a compulsory, basic 'service' module for students studying on a variety of life and environmental science courses. The students have not chosen to study chemistry and usually have a limited background in it; some have been intimidated by previous encounters with chemistry and many are frightened by the maths involved. In the 1980s, the course had fewer than 100 students on it, but this number had risen to over 200 by the mid-1990s. Peter Grebenik, the module leader, narrates the story.

PART 1

It was the end of the term in 1996, and I was entering the marks for the module. As the numbers of students in the module had grown, I had done one small thing to help me cope with the extra workload: I had stopped filling in the university's standard marksheet pro forma by hand. Instead, I had set up an equivalent computerized marksheet using Microsoft Excel and had developed and agreed with our student administration office a protocol for returning marks in electronic format to the university's student management system. Hardly revolutionary stuff! But it meant I was sitting at my computer entering the exam marks when I started to notice something about the marks.

Very few of the students had chosen or been able to successfully tackle a relatively simple chemical calculation. I began to reflect on my experience of the course and realized that I felt particularly uneasy about the problem class tutorials. In 1996, when the developments described in the case began, the course comprised a mixture of standard lectures, laboratory (practical) classes and small tutorial groups (12–15 students) in which the work was based on problem sheets that the students were instructed to attempt before the tutorial. The trouble with the tutorials was that too many of the students were frightened by the mathematics in the problem sheets and did not even look at the problems in advance because they knew they could 'hide' behind the few who did. Many of the classes turned into mini-lectures, and most students clearly made little effort to master the numerically based material – hence the poor performance on the numerical problems in the exam. This really bothered me, because the students were obviously not developing an important skill that they would need if they wanted to apply chemical ideas to their own subject areas. But how could I get all the students to attempt the problems?

What different methods do you think could be used to get students to try the problems?
What method do you think was actually tried?

PART 2

My first thought was that the only way to get the students to do the problems would be to attach marks to the work. At that time, assessment of the course was through writing up of practicals and a final exam consisting of multiple-choice questions and two longer problems. The idea of marking problems attempted by over 200 students made my hair stand up. Besides, in this type of work it would be difficult to prevent or detect collusion and copying among the students. But sitting at a computer with an Excel spreadsheet in front of me gave me an idea. 'What if I give the students an Excel spreadsheet on which to enter their solutions and which would also automatically mark their efforts?'

As soon as I finished entering the exam marks, I set about developing the detail of how this might work. I decided to create a template spreadsheet in which problems with numerical inputs could be individualized with different numerical values using the spreadsheet random number generator. This would allow the easy creation of a different spreadsheet for every student, thus preventing direct sharing of answers. The spreadsheet would indicate to the student whether he or she had the correct answer for each question attempted, thereby giving immediate feedback. I also inserted a cell in which an increasing number of letters of an individualized 'success code' would appear as more questions were successfully answered. I could use this unique success code to allocate marks. I decided to put 30 questions in the sheet (ensuring that students would have to attempt six questions on each of five question types). Students would be allowed to have as many attempts as they wanted, making it possible for them to get full marks if they persevered. To encourage student participation, I would allocate 10 per cent of the overall module assessment to these problems.

This scheme looked good to me, but I could imagine how threatening it might appear to some of the students. How would they cope with it? It was with some trepidation that I implemented my plan when the module ran the following year (1997). After exhaustive testing to remove 'bugs', I produced the problem spreadsheets using an Excel macro and then e-mailed each student his or her problem sheet as an attached file. I set a deadline for the work and told the students that they had to e-mail their own success code to me before the deadline. In view of my previous experience, I told the students that they had to get a minimum mark of 30 per cent on the spreadsheet. Otherwise, they would automatically fail the module even if they scored well on the exam. I also replaced the small group problem classes with a 'surgery' system for those students who needed extra help.

How did this mixture of 'carrots' and 'sticks' work? Out of the class of 260 students, 149 successfully completed all the questions on the spreadsheet, two students got less than 30 per cent and seven students did not attempt the spreadsheet at all. In the evaluation of the module, most students reported finding the spreadsheet one of the best things in it! What a relief!

Although not many students had attended the surgeries, the sessions were considered useful for those who needed them, and we made substantial savings in staff time by replacing the large number of relatively ineffective small group sessions with the surgeries.

I was very pleased with the overall result, but there still were a few problems. Most significantly, it had been very time consuming e-mailing out 260 separate files to students and entering the success codes from 253 students by hand. A 'dilemma' of an entirely different sort was that students tended to obtain high marks on the spreadsheet problems and this led to a substantial increase in the average mark for the module. Introductory Chemistry moved from being one of the lowest scoring first-year modules to the highest! Was there a risk of 'grade inflation' here?

The next year (1998), I modified the spreadsheet-assessed work in three important ways. First, I introduced a second and more difficult set of questions to increase the spread of marks and 'stretch' the better students. Second, I developed a very user-friendly method by which the students downloaded their own spreadsheet without the use of e-mail. And third, I programmed the spreadsheet so that each time it was saved to disk, it wrote a summary of student performance to a remote file, thus saving all the effort of having to enter the success codes by hand. Although students found the second set of problems quite demanding (average mark of 56 per cent compared to an average mark of 91 per cent on the easier problem set), student evaluations of the spreadsheet problems remained very positive.

I was feeling pretty good about what had happened so far. The spreadsheet approach had solved the problem of making students tackle simple numerical problems, and it gave them both instant feedback and some reward for their efforts. But I was still left with one major dilemma: the method appeared to be appropriate for only certain portions of the module content. Was there some way I could adapt my method to encourage students to actively engage with the remaining, more descriptive parts of chemistry?

What different methods do you think could be used to get students to engage with the descriptive parts of chemistry to the same extent that they were now doing with the numerical problems?
What method do you think was actually tried?

PART 3

By coincidence, during that year I attended a workshop on computer-assisted assessment run by the university's academic development unit. One of the highlights of the day for me was when we participants were able to try out some software designed to create simple Web-based multiple-choice question (MCQ) tests that gave instant feedback. The software was so simple to use that in less than half an hour I had managed to create a test with 10 questions in it. That's when it struck me: if it was this easy, I could create a set of questions for each week of the Introductory Chemistry course. The students could attempt them in their own time and thereby gain instant feedback on how well they had understood that week's topic. But how could I persuade students (other than the very enthusiastic ones) to work on the questions? I didn't want to attach any more marks to coursework on this module, and anyway it would be far too easy for students to collude, as it wasn't possible to individualize the MCQ tests with the software I proposed to use.

I raised this issue with Chris, who ran the session. When I told him that the end-of-term exam included MCQs, he suggested that I put some of the weekly practice questions in the end-of-term exam. Then if I told the students about this arrangement, surely they would be motivated to work on them, without having to give any marks! I found this idea very attractive and decided to give it a go.

When I ran the module again in 1999, it was significantly different. In addition to the two spreadsheets (now worth a total of 15 per cent of the marks for the module), and the practical work (also worth 15 per cent), each week there was available an unassessed Web-based MCQ test. I told the students that 5 out of the 20 questions set each week would appear on the final exam. With eight of these weekly tests available, this gave assiduous students the chance to try no fewer than 40 of the 80 final exam MCQs prior to the exam, although they had to do all 160 in-course MCQs to achieve this. I was worried that this might lead to an excessive increase in the average mark for the module, so I told the students right at the outset that some form of negative marking would be applied in the exam as the *quid pro quo* for half the exam being 'seen'.

For a while as I started preparing the Web-based MCQ tests, I had severe workload problems and wondered whether I would be able to keep up with the demands. Even starting with a bank of 80 questions, I found it hard to generate enough new questions for the weekly tests – writing a mere four new questions was good going for a two-hour work session. However, I managed to stay ahead of the class – barely.

For the negative marking on the final exam, I decided to subtract 0.2 mark for each wrong answer in a 'choose one from five' MCQ. When the exam had been completed and marked, I found that for the 40 exam questions that had also been present on the weekly Web-based tests, 59 per cent of responses were correct, 28 per cent were wrong, and the remaining 13 per cent were left blank. For the 40 unseen questions, the corresponding percentages were 42, 36 and 22. In the previous year, when there was no negative marking and students had been encouraged to put a response (even a complete guess) for all questions, 44 per cent of responses were correct and 56 per cent were wrong. Whatever else these results might mean (the seen and unseen questions had not been randomized on the exam), they suggested at least that many of the students had gone through the weekly practice tests.

There were two unexpected consequences of this regime. Compared to the previous year, 'good' students or ones who had worked hard on the practice tests got higher scores in the exam, while 'poor' or less committed students scored less well, due to negative marking. This was reflected in a 50 per cent increase in the standard deviation on the exam mark. A benefit to myself from negative marking came from examining those questions that many students had chosen not to attempt, as these indicated areas of the course in which students had developed little confidence, and that therefore needed to be taught differently.

I kept all of these innovations when I ran the module again in 2000, but I introduced two further refinements. The first was that I made all the weekly MCQ practice tests available from the very start of the module. The second was to meet a niggling worry I had that the negative marking of the MCQs in the final exam was equally punitive per question to the student who was 'genuinely' wrong and the student who was just wildly guessing. I implemented a sliding scale of negative marking using what I call the 'guess ratio', calculated for each student from the number of wrong answers and the number of questions attempted. The whole system is based on the premise that a student who knows nothing and always guesses deserves to score zero. The students accepted its rationale as fair. It certainly led to a wide range of deductions for incorrect responses among the students (a fourfold difference in the size of the deduction factor over the whole class), but did it *really* deal with my concern as I had intended? I don't know. I am concerned by a trend showing a rise in the proportion of unanswered questions in my MCQ exams in which students are told that there will be negative marking.

Overall, the results I obtained from the innovations I tried suggest that strategic use of various computer applications can both reduce staff workload (ignoring the development overhead) and increase student learning. In particular, these applications have motivated and enabled students to structure work in their own time, and have permitted them to make repeated efforts to get work right in an anonymous risk-free environment where initial wrong answers will not show them up in front of their peers or teachers.

What do you think of the various IT assessment applications that were employed?
What are the lessons from the case for your own assessment practice?

CASE REPORTERS' DISCUSSION

Thank goodness for IT! That is something that both the students and faculty involved could conclude from the experiences reported in the case. The judicious application of IT allowed a number of seemingly intractable problems in a large introductory chemistry course to be at least partially resolved. Arguably most important was the encouragement it gave to students to tackle mathematical problems in chemistry that previous cohorts had avoided attempting out of fear or insecurity. By allowing students an unlimited number of attempts and by giving them immediate feedback on their answers, the spreadsheet method gave students the confidence they needed to engage with the problems.

At the same time, there were distinct benefits for faculty. They were able to give students in a large introductory course individualized formative feedback without major ongoing expenditure of time or effort. For the mathematical problem sets, creating and marking a series of unique spreadsheets was almost totally automated, requiring only minimal staff time. Furthermore, the hardware and software requirements for such a programme were fairly basic. Since the only software required for the spreadsheet was Microsoft Excel, the problem sets were easy to construct and students who had a computer at home could take their problem sheets home on a floppy disk and work on them there.

The further application of IT to the more descriptive, theory part of the course also proved useful to both students and teachers. Once again, students were able to get formative feedback on their progress in this part of the course. The 'carrot' of allowing the students to have a 'partially seen' MCQ final exam was sufficient inducement for the majority of students to use the Web-based formative assessment questions without having any marks or credit attached to them. While one could debate the necessity of incorporating negative marking for incorrect answers in the final MCQ exam as 'the *quid pro quo*' for half of it being 'seen', it certainly discouraged guessing and teachers were enabled to identify areas of the course where students lacked confidence or where teaching could be improved, by noting questions that were left unanswered by substantial numbers of students.

Finally, the case provides a good example of course development that is responsive to new issues, previous experience and changing circumstances. The module leader and the course itself moved a long way from merely doing away with hand entry of marks to the provision of opportunities for automated, individualized formative feedback to each of some 260 students. Each stage in the evolution built on those that had gone before and, the module leader's insecurity and worry about each new step notwithstanding, each of them was carefully enough thought out and well enough supported by sound educational principles that it had a good prospect of succeeding.

CHAPTER 3

GAIN WITHOUT PAIN?

Case reporter: Peter Schwartz

Issues raised

This case study raises issues associated with moving from formal, end-of-course assessment to much more regular quizzes of learning for a large class. An important consideration throughout is the attitude of teaching staff towards change.

Background

The University of Otago Medical School is the older of the two medical schools in New Zealand. It is a public institution and was founded in 1875. It had for many years a traditional curriculum based on the British system. Class size has been around 190 students per year in recent years. Most students come from privileged backgrounds. Immediately after completing secondary school, most students do a one-year preparatory course for the health sciences, following which they enter the medical course. Teaching staff numbers are around 275–300, supplemented by a large number of clinicians.

PART 1

Okay – so how were we going to satisfy both sides? The students were saying: 'We want more opportunity to test our understanding', and 'We want more feedback on our progress', and 'We want credit for the work we're doing during the year and we don't want everything to be based on a final exam.' But the teachers were saying: 'We're already doing too much teaching and with everything else that the University expects us to do, we can't spend any more time on activities related to teaching.'

It was the mid-1990s. The University of Otago Medical School was preparing to introduce an integrated, modular, systems-based pre-clinical curriculum to replace a traditional curriculum that had been in place for many years. Faculty members had recently rejected a proposal to adopt problem-based learning (PBL) for the pre-clinical curriculum, many teachers refusing to look at the evidence about PBL or even to recognize that the old curriculum needed improvement. In addition, the University administration was widely perceived as failing to give adequate recognition to teaching in deciding such matters as promotion or study leave. Understandably, then, most faculty were unwilling to devote time and effort to improving teaching.

At the time, I was chairing a small working party that was given the task of preparing proposals for assessing student performance in the new curriculum. In attempting to satisfy the requests of both students and teachers, we had a number of issues to consider: the medical class was large; the numbers of teachers were relatively small; resources were not abundant; there was no dedicated medical education support unit and little local expertise upon which to draw. On top of that, the University administration was in the process of issuing new guidelines on assessment. Of most interest to us were the recommendations that formative assessment be given at least as much emphasis as summative assessment, that assessment tasks of all sorts be given credit, and that feedback on assessment be given to students promptly.

It looked like a tall order to come up with something that would meet all the requirements – but we *were* introducing a new curriculum that we felt would be an improvement on the old one and we *should* have a new assessment system to complement it. The question was: what form should it take?

If you were faced with this decision, what assessment methods would you consider?
What methods do you think were actually selected?

PART 2

In the old curriculum, most assessment was summative, end-of-course, and based on testing recall of information. Essay and short answer questions were favoured, but a few disciplines used multiple-choice questions. Students had little or no opportunity to get feedback on their progress during the course. We on the assessment-design working party believed that there must be a better assessment system. Fortunately, several of us were not just enthusiasts: we were in a position to try out alternatives in our own courses in order to develop ideas for the new programme-wide assessment system. Together with some of my colleagues, I tried a paper-based system of quizzes in our course in clinical biochemistry. Questions required application of information and/or problem solving, but only very brief answers were necessary. Two versions of each quiz were available, so students who failed to reach the designated 'pass' level on the first attempt could have another opportunity. All students took a quiz at the same time. Meanwhile, Andy, another member of the assessment-design group, trialled a totally computerized system of quizzing in anatomic pathology. The goals and many of the methods of his trial were similar to those in the paper-based trial, but, in pathology, the students took the quizzes individually at times that suited them. Each question on a pathology quiz was prepared in three versions and students got one of these versions at random on the first attempt. In each of the trials, successful completion of the quizzes conferred some credit toward the final mark for the course.

Both methods proved enormously popular with the students. They really liked getting feedback on their progress, the chance to retake failed quizzes, the stimulus provided by the regular quizzing to keep up with their coursework, and the opportunity to obtain credit for work done during the course. We on the assessment-design working party seemed to be in the happy position of having at least two successful options to choose from!

At a meeting of the assessment group where we were to make a choice, I said: 'Our paper-based trial worked really well. The way we set out the questions, they were quick and easy to mark, even by hand – and we got the whole class through in one go.' Andy responded: 'Yes, but you know that the teaching staff are already complaining about spending too much time teaching. Even if it took you – what? – a couple of hours to mark the papers from the whole class, who would agree to do that on a regular basis? That wasn't a problem with our computer-based tests. They were scored by the computer on the spot and the students got feedback on their answers immediately.' 'Besides', Tony added, ' you had to get the whole class together to give the quiz. You want to do that for testing in the whole new curriculum?' I had to agree with them and (reluctantly) accept that it was time to enter the Information Technology era if we wanted to accomplish our goals.

Eventually, my working party prepared a proposal for regular, in-course computerized testing as an integral part of the new curriculum for the two pre-clinical years of the medical course. During each integrated module, students would take quizzes each covering, on average, two to three weeks of material. The format would be 'modified mastery', so students would be able to take up to two additional, alternative versions of any quiz that they failed. Feedback on answers would be provided on the spot, and failing students would have the opportunity to obtain remedial help. Upon successful completion of the quizzes, students would receive a fixed percentage credit toward their final mark for the year. The programme of in-course assessment would be supplemented by a series of integrated, case-based final examinations requiring written answers. These would determine the major part of each student's mark for the year and would serve mainly to rank students.

We were pleased with our proposal, as was the faculty group responsible for implementing the new curriculum. Although questions were raised about the number of times students should be allowed to retake quizzes and whether it was appropriate for credit towards the final mark to be given for students having passed the quizzes, the implementation group approved the proposal and both the hardware and the staff support to mount the testing programme were forthcoming.

Meanwhile, with some changes in membership, my assessment working party was transformed into a 'vetting' team to review the questions that teachers were proposing to include in the quizzes for their modules. Although in the final analysis we had little authority over the content of the assessments in the individual modules, we were working on the premise (and tried to convince those submitting questions to accept the premise) that the quizzes would be the backbone of assessment in the new curriculum – or, as a clinical colleague suggested, that they would allow teachers to certify that students had a 'warrant of fitness' at the end of a module. I was firmly convinced that the quizzes would provide the best opportunity for teachers to ensure that students were able to do what teachers wanted them to do by the end of each module. The final exams, with their limited scope for 'sampling' the content of each module, would clearly not be as useful for this purpose. And since faculty members had accepted the precepts of the new curriculum (one of which stated that 'teaching and assessment should focus on principles, with details given less emphasis'), surely we could expect interesting, well thought out, high quality questions for the new quizzes.

Imagine my dismay when, with some notable exceptions, many of the submitted questions – regardless of their format – required nothing more than outright recognition of factual material, much of it highly detailed. We agonized over the situation. I said to my colleagues: 'I don't think we should accept these. They're junk. They don't at all fit with what we're trying to do.' Dave said: 'I don't think we have much choice. We've already asked faculty to do a lot of work preparing for the new curriculum. If we reject their questions, they might just rebel and refuse to submit any questions at all. At least this way we'll have something and, once the workload settles back to normal, we can work with them to improve the questions.' I responded: 'I accept your point, but my fear is that, once the questions are in place and being used, people will sit back and say: "We've done that now" and they'll show little initiative in improving them. I'm not happy about the questions.'

What would you advise the 'vetting' team to do about the questions being submitted?
What would you do next?
What do you think actually happened?

PART 3

The computerized in-course assessment programme has now been in place for four years. The format has stayed as originally proposed, with very few modifications. Logistically, it has run extremely well. The students have been very enthusiastic about the regular opportunities to test themselves and obtain feedback, about the stimulus provided by the quizzes to keep up with their studies, and about the chance to obtain credit toward their final marks from the small, relatively non-threatening quizzes. Teachers have been pleased to be able to give the students more feedback without having to spend time themselves testing or marking.

Regrettably, however, the gain has not been painless. As I feared, many of the questions are (and have remained) of poor quality. Most teachers have shown little inclination to modify or improve their questions or to emulate the few good examples. Some questions and even entire sections of some quizzes have been roundly condemned by the students as testing trivia or excessive detail, or as not reflecting the emphasis of the relevant module. Teachers respond by claiming that they can test only the most basic factual material in the computerized format – again without looking at examples from our own tests or from elsewhere that demonstrate otherwise.

The fact that, once submitted, the questions become part of a centralized testing programme out of the direct sight or control of teachers in the module has complicated things further. Although module convenors are advised at the end of each year of the students' performance on each item in the module's quizzes, there is not much incentive to act on the information provided. While being relieved of much of the *burden* associated with assessment, the convenors seem also to take less *responsibility for* assessment in the new system. This phenomenon was brought home particularly force-fully on one occasion when a new lecturer was brought into a module after another teacher had taught and provided assessment items for the relevant part for two years. The new teacher taught the material he considered important, but neither he nor the module team ever checked that what was being assessed matched what was being taught. They did not match and, after complaints from the students, the quiz in question was made voluntary rather than required.

In an effort finally to make some progress on improving the assessments, we obtained Faculty support for summer studentships for several students who have completed the new pre-clinical curriculum to review the quizzes, designed an instrument for evaluating the quality of questions, and worked with teachers to improve weak questions. We are hopeful that their work will generate momentum to strengthen the quizzes. In the meantime, the medical student classes as a whole have unilaterally taken their own steps. We understand that for those questions and quizzes that the students feel are asking about irrelevant or excessively 'picky' factual detail, some students who are taking the quizzes early are advising the rest about what the questions and answers are – thus totally subverting the 'testing' function of the quiz. On those quizzes that they deem relevant and fair, they are not sharing the questions and answers, regardless of the extent of the challenge posed by the questions.

Our use of computerized testing for a large class of medical students has so far shown great promise, but it has thrown up some challenges as well. We look forward to working with our students to meet those challenges so that our plan for in-course assessment can finally match fully our original intentions for it.

What do you think of the outcome?
What other steps might have been taken to overcome some of the problems experienced?
What lessons are there for others from this case?

CASE REPORTER'S DISCUSSION

The goal of developing an assessment system for a large class that would meet the dual aims of offering students more opportunities for testing themselves and for obtaining feedback while at the same time *not* requiring more time and effort from teachers is one that is probably quite widely shared. Hence the lessons we learnt as we tried to meet the various challenges may be of use to others as well as ourselves.

We concluded that, given our circumstances, computerization was the best way to achieve the aims, but, as we discovered, it is not a guarantee of immediate, complete success, nor is it the easy, painless option that some teachers seem to think it is. In our experience, having high quality hardware and good staff support for programming assessment items and actually running the computerized testing were extremely valuable – but they did not obviate the need for teachers to devote time and effort to designing good questions and to monitoring the assessments once they had been prepared. As reported in the case study, this is the weakest part of our development to date. And it is here that we must attack the problem. At the simplest and most pragmatic level, we could try to convince teachers that if they spend the time and effort to get things right *once*, the testing programme will be able to run successfully without much further input from them for the next several years. However, this apparently simple solution to a highly specific problem is complicated by the need to consider some of the widely applicable principles for successfully introducing educational change. We shall have to consider them more carefully if we want to make progress, and it is their involvement in our story that provides what are probably the most important lessons for others from our experience.

From our perspective, two of these principles (and their attendant corollaries) are particularly relevant. The first is **the crucial need for faculty who are to be involved in designing and monitoring assessment items to understand and fully 'buy into' the system**, including its underlying philosophy. We simply have not fully accomplished this yet. For once, unlike for other proposed educational changes at our medical school, we had no trouble convincing teachers of the potential benefits of the proposed change – there seemed to be benefits for the students at little or no apparent 'cost' to teachers. However, merely adopting the method is not enough. Teachers also have to understand and accept the philosophy. Few of our teachers either understand or see the reason for implementing the 'warrant of fitness' concept for the in-course assessments. Until they do, there is little likelihood that we shall develop uniformly good assessment items. Hence, a corollary to this important principle is the need to have an effective faculty development programme available. Our teachers need to have the opportunity to develop greater insight into the purposes of assessment and into the construction of good assessment items.

Once teachers have gained this insight, they have to use it to prepare good assessment items and then maintain an interest in monitoring and refining them. This will require time and effort. The second important principle from our experience, therefore, is that **there must be incentives of some sort for teachers to do the work to prepare good assessment items**. In our situation, teachers do not perceive any potential benefits other than the intrinsic satisfaction of doing a good job. In fact, for many teachers, convening a module and being responsible for all that that entails (including assessment) is seen as a burden that interferes with their ability to engage in activities that are perceived to be rewarded. Again, until the University or the Medical School develops some method to recognize the effort associated with preparing good assessment items, we are unlikely to have an optimal system of assessment.

Finally, what could we have done differently? Well, other than applying the principles I have just enumerated, we could have rejected the poor quality questions right from the start – and then possibly we would have had to find someone or some group with the authority to force compliance for the good of the curriculum when the overworked teachers refused to conform. I suspect, however, that the overall result to date would not have been any better than it is.

CHAPTER 4

WHAT TO DO ABOUT JOHN?

Case reporter: Sally Brown

Issues raised

This case explores issues associated with devising and setting effective computer-assisted assessment tests.

Background

I am an external adviser on assessment to a number of universities in the United Kingdom and internationally. Several are putting a lot of energy and resources into developing computer-assisted assessment (CAA) for both formative and summative purposes. The incidents described in the case are an aggregation of events that took place at several UK universities, and the character I am calling John is a typical faculty member, having been encouraged to use CAA without having had much in the way of previous experience or training in its use.

PART 1

What to do about John? Like most of the other faculty at the university, he was keen and he was more than happy to go along with the move to develop and use CAA. The problem was that he hadn't had any previous experience with it, and he also hadn't had any training in developing good assessment items. This might not have been much of a problem, but he also 'knew all the answers'.

The university has a great deal of expertise, both technical and pedagogic, on CAA, but in this instance my advice had been sought on generic assessment issues, not specifically on techniques for CAA. Indeed, I learnt a great deal from the university about how to implement CAA effectively and developmentally with large groups of students from a wide variety of backgrounds. The support and facilities they provide for staff, the training they provide on designing CAA tests for those who wish to take it up, the facilities they offer for the implementation of the tests, and the thought they put into issues such as security and authenticity are unparalleled.

I was asked particularly to look at CAA tests in a number of subjects in which the items had been produced by the lecturers involved. Some of these faculty were very experienced in producing CAA materials, but others were relative novices. All staff implementing CAA were asked to provide a breakdown of the types of outcomes that they expected each question to assess, using Bloom's taxonomy as the basis of this evaluation. My task was to play with the questions and to comment on both the question types and whether they were actually testing the kinds of outcomes they claimed to test.

The vast majority of the tests I looked at were extremely well produced, using a variety of question formats in creative ways. However, one tutor in particular, John, who was teaching first-year students in a hard sciences course, was producing tests that were less than successful.

On most of the tests that I examined, being unfamiliar with the subject material, I was able to do little more than look at the wording of the questions and the kinds of responses that were sought. However, I found that on one particular test that John had prepared – a test in which the questions were all straight 'pick one answer from five' multiple-choice questions – I was fairly readily able to guess the correct option. Indeed, many of the questions were so worded that the correct option was obvious. For example, four of the distractors (wrong options) would be relatively short and the key (correct option) was the longest. (I was able to check this was indeed the right option as, usefully, details of the correct choices were provided for me.)

Furthermore, where the question asked for choice among a number of causes for an effect, guessing that the right option was the one that contained the most complex-sounding information generally helped me to hit the jackpot. I could also guess the right option where the question asked for multiple interdependent causes rather than a single cause and where all the options, except one, contained a negative. I could also do quite well by opting for 'all of the above' or 'none of the above' when these options were included. By pure guesswork and native cunning, and with absolutely no knowledge of the subject matter, I did pretty well on the test, scoring 57 per cent – considerably higher than the 20 per cent I should have expected to get randomly in a well-designed five-option test.

Another problem associated with John's evaluation of the test was that he claimed that analysis, synthesis and evaluation were being tested, whereas, in my opinion, the test was primarily seeking subject recall.

This looked like a slightly tricky situation. I was faced with a faculty member who was preparing questions that were not nearly of as high quality as I generally found at the university. Furthermore, the lecturer believed that the items were testing larger numbers of topics and higher levels of abilities than I did. I had been asked to advise, so what should I do?

Should I:

a) give up and write this particular lecturer off?
b) demand that John discard all his questions because they were rubbish?
c) hint to John's head of department or dean that John was incompetent and should be fired?
d) suggest to John that he abandon the use of CAA?
e) none of the above?

If you were the consultant in this case, what would you do next?
What do you think actually happened next?

PART 2

Just as for some of the items that I had inspected, the facetious multiple-choice set of options has only one reasonable answer: 'none of the above'. I wanted to help John develop insight into how to prepare CAA questions that were as good as those I found elsewhere at the university. I suggested to John that his test would be better able to suit its purposes if he were to rethink what it was that he was attempting to achieve and also if he were able to learn about the wide range of question types available from many colleagues at the university.

There is a considerable amount of expertise in question design for CAA in the hard sciences and its best proponents choose to mix question types which:

- seek best-match answers;
- ask students to click on-screen hotspots to identify relevant points on graphs;
- get students to click on a series of arrows to demonstrate correct pathways on diagrams;
- require students to select and position labels for elements of graphs, charts or diagrams;
- ask students to put some given factors into an order of importance;

and so on, rather than just using simple multiple-choice questions.

John, however, was unconvinced, viewing the syllabus as containing a lot of facts which needed to be remembered by the students, and believing that simple multiple-choice questions would suffice to test this. He believed that all that was needed was to devise questions to find out what the students remembered of the content of the syllabus. John thus had an orientation towards teaching that favoured 'content-centred' approaches rather than 'learning-centred' approaches, with the focus on the material that is taught rather than on the student or on ensuring that learning takes place. He also believed that I had been very lucky with my guesses! The problem was thus not just a technical one involving question design but a more fundamental one of values and intent. It looked like I had a real dilemma to sort out. How could John be helped to 'see the light'?

What steps would you take to help John develop greater insight into the design of appropriate test items?
What do you think actually happened?

PART 3

John was at a meeting of staff involved in CAA that I attended. The topic of poor question design was raised and I indicated that I had significant concerns. John became very agitated and informed the group that he had put a lot of time and energy into developing the tests, and he was not prepared to be pilloried for what he had done. He had, however, been quite shocked to discover how well I had done on his test by guesswork. In due course, he calmed down.

The Chair of the meeting sought proposals for future action for the whole group. It was agreed that there should be further staff development work-shops in which the staff of the university could share good practice. They agreed to sample questions on each other's tests prior to the next run and also to collectively explore the literature on the topic.

Piloting of questions with 'live' students was also considered important and several of those present agreed to explore piloting some actual exam questions during the pre-test 'taster' sessions, which are used to acclimatize students to what is for them a new assessment format – since multiple-choice testing is not as common in the United Kingdom as it is in a number of other countries.

These steps all sounded good to me, but I left the meeting wondering whether John really was likely to change his ideas or his methods as a result. Only time would tell.

What do you think of the outcome?
What other steps might have been taken to help John?

CASE REPORTER'S DISCUSSION

Although it has been reported as a problem occurring with an individual lecturer in the context of preparing good test items for CAA, the case raises a number of key issues that apply to the implementation of almost any innovative educational approach. They are particularly relevant to the introduction of innovative assessment practices like CAA and may well have influenced what happened in the case.

First and foremost is the issue of **the management of change**. The developments in CAA at the university described occurred when individuals decided voluntarily to attempt something new as part of an institutional initiative. Their reasons for volunteering were varied, from the saving of staff time to the belief that CAA afforded more and better opportunities to give students feedback on their performance. However, despite attempts by the university's teaching development centre to promote a strategic shift towards implementation of CAA, the approach was taken up mainly by 'lone heroes' who were sometimes working in a vacuum. This is unlikely to be the best method of bringing about widespread change in an organization, but it is difficult to balance the need to manage change strategically and the need to foster and encourage individuals who are enthusiastic about implementing innovations but who may sometimes end up 'reinventing the wheel' or making heavy weather of something that a team might tackle better. In the context of the case, it is difficult to know whether John's questions would have been better if he had developed them as part of a team, but his working on his own left his questions totally vulnerable to his inexperience and lack of knowledge about either CAA or the design of good assessment items.

A second crucial issue is that of **appropriate staff development for the implementation of innovation**. The university had provided lots of workshops on both the practical and technical aspects of CAA, including effective question design, and there was much relevant expertise available at the teaching development centre. But staff were not required to attend such training, nor was there any institutional requirement to demonstrate competence in CAA development before starting to use it. In fact, it is hard to see how such a requirement could have been introduced, since it is difficult enough to get enthusiasts to become involved in innovation without putting bureaucratic barriers in their way. The question remains, however, whether it is appropriate to leave question design to amateurs – and in this regard John was an amateur, never having taken advantage of the training in CAA. Perhaps he will be stimulated to make use of the university's resources as a result of the meeting described in Part 3, but it remains to be seen.

Next, and of especial relevance to the design and use of assessment items, is the issue of **quality assurance**. In contexts where multiple-choice testing is commonplace, it is the norm to require extensive piloting and testing of questions before their use with students in real summative exams. However, where CAA tests are designed for small groups of students on an annual or semi-annual basis, it is difficult to see how this could be undertaken by individual lecturers in any manageable fashion. Trials of sample questions in pre-test 'tasters' can be used to enhance the skills of those designing tests and can at least make CAA developers aware in practice of faults in question design they learnt about in the staff development sessions. Feedback from students on why they chose particular answers can be extremely illuminating to question designers and can help to improve future CAA tests. This of course needs to be planned from the outset. We can but hope that John joins his colleagues in the pilot trials of CAA items.

One of the huge potential benefits of CAA is the possibility of giving **formative feedback** quickly on correct and incorrect responses by providing a screen of text including explanations of right and wrong answers. This moves CAA from a testing to a learning tool and can dramatically improve student performance. However, it adds a whole new dimension to the problems facing the writers of assessment items: it is very time consuming and 'uses up' questions that cannot readily be reused in summative assessment. It is, nevertheless, a feature of the best available CAA systems, and a proposal to use CAA in this way can help to convince those uncertain about the approach of the value of using technology to support learning. The possibility of building formative feedback into summative tests can usefully be explored in those institutions in which CAA is being implemented on a substantial scale. John was an enthusiast for CAA from the outset, so if he can be convinced to attend workshops at which he can learn more about it, he might well be supportive of the notion of using CAA to provide formative feedback to students – in addition to being able to write better questions.

Finally, it is worth considering the value of someone like myself, acting as an 'external eye', in helping faculty to develop their skills in an area as innovative, sensitive and demanding of high quality as the appropriate application of CAA. My role as external adviser at the university described in the case has not always made me popular, but I think it has been helpful because I am able to:

- look at CAA tests from an outsider's point of view, emulating to some extent the students' experience, even though I am a non-specialist in the subject matter;
- advise on the balance of different types of question used and comment when the design of the test overall is repetitive, tedious, dull or impractical;
- scrutinize the test designer's analysis of the test's coverage of topics and levels of questions and comment on their balance; and
- sample tests to see whether guessing and native cunning have an inappropriate pay-off.

It has been an extremely useful two-way process. I have learnt a tremendous amount about the technicalities of CAA and I feel that my advice on assessment issues has been beneficial to the team involved – although perhaps not to every individual within it! Just ask John. But then maybe he'd give a different answer in a couple of years if he responds to what I and his colleagues have been saying.

REFLECTIVE ASSESSMENT: JOURNALS, LOGBOOKS, PORTFOLIOS, PEER ASSESSMENT

CHAPTER 5

ASSESSING REFLECTION OR SUPPORTING LEARNING?

Case reporter: Lorraine Stefani

Issues raised

This case considers how to go about encouraging students to reflect on their learning and to value self-evaluation even when these activities do not contribute towards their grade.

Background

Energy Systems and the Environment is a postgraduate programme offered by the Faculty of Engineering at the University of Strathclyde in the UK. The course is primarily concerned with the design and operation of the systems that control the environment in which people live and work. Part A of the programme is the foundation studies section, addressing principles and issues that underpin all energy systems; Part B is the special studies section, during which students undertake a group-based design project over an interval of 12 weeks; and Part C requires an individual thesis on an environmental theme. There are 20–30 students per class. Many of the students in the class are international students, mature students or both.

PART 1

Hmm! – maybe I should have continued working with genes rather than engineers! I had taken up the position of Lecturer in the Centre for Academic Practice at the University of Strathclyde in 1994. This was a change of career for me as previously I had been a Lecturer in Human Genetics at the Queen's University, Belfast. On taking up my new position, I was somewhat surprised to find that essentially I had to create my own job! It wasn't that there was a shortage of work – it was more a case of making sure people in the University would actually know of my existence. So I generally said yes to any request and hoped I would be able to deliver in a reasonable manner whatever was being requested. One day I received a telephone call from a professor in mechanical engineering. He said: 'I'm fascinated by the idea of learning journals. I'd like you to encourage my students to each keep one.' 'Whoa!', I thought, 'learning journals for engineers – that's a tall order!' As he described it, my role would be to encourage the students during Part B of the programme to 'keep a learning journal' – initially for no other obvious (to the students) reason than that the professor in charge of the programme liked the idea! I was painfully aware how difficult this could be, given that engineering students are often the recipients of traditional chalk and talk teaching methods, and the idea of jotting down their reflections was unlikely to inspire them. However, I felt I had no choice but to give it a try and I was intrigued by the possibility that I could enhance student learning in the process. But how in the world could I meet such a challenge?

What would you do in this situation?
What do you think actually happened?

PART 2

For the part of the programme that would involve the journal, the class was divided into groups of four or five students engaged on a major project. My initial idea was to use the group project as the lever for reflection. What I did in the first instance was to try to get the students on my side! I thought that if I gave them some input to support them in their group task, perhaps they would feel more favourably disposed to this 'fancy notion' of a learning journal. So I spent a few workshop sessions helping the students to under-stand the complexities of group work and to gain more insight into both the task and the process elements of the project. I was in no doubt that the students did actually value these sessions, so I was hopeful about the journal.

During this first run of the exercise, I borrowed a model from the arts and social sciences and I suggested that the group should simply keep a free flow journal recording different stages of their project. Around half the students did keep an individual journal and they used it mainly to let off steam about the inadequacies of their team members. The journals may just have been therapeutic for some individuals!

However, there was a fairly immediate problem. While on the one hand the Engineering professor was fascinated by the concept of learning journals, he was not fascinated enough to give the journal any weight in the course's assessment. This meant that students who had made the effort were peeved that they gained no extra credit for keeping the journal. I did read the journals and give feedback, but the students felt a bit conned by it all – just as I would have predicted.

The next time I ran the exercise, I tried to take the issue a step further by redefining what I was trying to encourage students to do. Instead of focusing on an individual learning journal, which did not have a lot of currency with the students, I proposed and designed a project management logbook. I believed that the group project held great potential for learning and for reflection on learning, so the redesigned logbook was tailored to a group approach and to reflection on both the task and the process elements of the group project – the idea being to make the link between the project and reflection on learning more transparent and more relevant to the students. A project must be managed and so the redesigned logbook was laid out to provide space to write about project stages, delegation of tasks, resources required, time management, etc. The intention was that the students would keep a group logbook and perhaps delegate the task of maintaining it to one of the group members. As before, I indulged in the sort of bribery and manipulation I've already described and I facilitated a series of workshops to help them in their project management.

So what happened this time? Different philosophy – same outcome. The issue of whether the journal/logbook should 'count' in assessment was still undecided. However, the professor stated that the logbook had to be handed in with the project dissertation. Given that the programme components were assessed on a pass/fail basis, smart students could work out that they were unlikely to fail just because they did not submit a project management logbook. I felt frustrated. I was not achieving my goal of encouraging students to reflect on their learning. There was a gap to be filled to convince students this was a worthwhile exercise. I was tempted to give up, but I believed this was important enough that I should persevere. But how could I improve my chances of success?

Why do you think the students were so resistant to keeping a logbook?
What steps would you recommend taking next?
What do you think actually happened?

PART 3

One of the reasons that I persisted with this project for so long was that I myself was keen to get the students to recognize the value of reflection. I was also aware that employers were becoming much keener on seeing students acquire the ability to engage in personal development and planning, so it seemed that the relevance of what I was trying to do was increasing all the time. Just like the professor, I had misgivings about applying summative assessment to something that, in essence, was 'owned' by the student or student group. So I felt that the real goals were to encourage reflection and to convince students of the value of self-evaluation or appraisal and of formative feedback where requested and where appropriate.

The next stage in the project proved extremely interesting. Over a period of a few years, it became fairly standard that around half the students would keep a logbook, whatever the format – and others would say: 'I wish I had kept a logbook because I can see now that it would have been beneficial.' The issue became how to capitalize on this realization. It was clear that the tide was turning and that the gap between what we were encouraging students to do and what was happening out in the 'real' world was closing. What came out of discussions between the professor and myself was that we should modernize the format for the group project. Why were we still asking students to present paper-based dissertations when in fact we could be capitalizing on the potential of new technologies?

We asked the students to present their project as a Web page and we gave them full support by organizing HTML workshops. We said also that the project management logbook should comprise a section of the Web page. I had been regularly reviewing what I was trying to do and I came to realize that if students truly took ownership of the logbook format, they might be more motivated to maintain logbooks.

I asked the next class of students working on their group project to use a series of guidelines to develop a part of their Web page as the basis of the project management logbook. The project and the logbook would then become a visible record of what they had done, what they had achieved and how they had achieved their outcomes. The guidelines were as follows:

1. Working in groups of four, prepare a brief for your group project assignment. Include in this brief the project title, a description of the project, the deadline for completion of the project and what resources will be needed.
2. Define the processes by which you as a group will carry out this project, eg delegation of tasks, skills required for completion, levels of commitment required from team members, what potential difficulties you perceive with the project, time management, etc.
3. Having defined your project and what skills, resources etc are required to successfully complete the project, as a group write how both the task and the processes in your assignment should be assessed and evaluated. In other words, what are your criteria for excellence in this project?

What happened as a result of these changes was quite remarkable. The student groups all presented details of their project planning. The idea of changing from paper-based formats to electronic formats clearly acted as a driving force for the class. Where previously the students had made oral presentations to industrial representatives at the end of the project, they were now able to present their work in a much more professional manner. Remarkably, the professionalization of the presentation also had an enormous impact on the students' willingness to maintain project management logbooks. It may be that the students could now see more clearly the value of project planning, of being able to present that planning and of being able to work towards their own conception of excellence within the project. It may also be that providing students with a coherent and meaningful framework for reflection was another factor in the success of this trial. Why it is worth writing about is that this format is now embedded within the postgraduate engineering programme and it has been found to be transferable to other subject areas.

What factors do you think were responsible for students' eventual acceptance of the project management logbooks?
What effect might further consideration of the issue of summative assessment of the logbooks have had?
What lessons does this case have for you in your own situation?

CASE REPORTER'S DISCUSSION

This project was enormously challenging, but over a period of a few years I feel I moved a long way. I started by simply asking students to keep a free-flow journal, recording their own progress. When this assignment proved just too unstructured, I moved to a pre-prepared logbook that I hoped would provide a framework for reflective learning that had some meaning for the students. The new format had guides and prompts on topics to be recorded, such as group skills, task management, etc. While the new style had more structure and gave more guidance, it failed because it gave the students insufficient 'ownership' of the format. In the final electronic group log, each group designed its own Web page and its own recording format to present its project management outline. This documented progress towards group-defined attainment targets, skill development, time management, unexpected difficulties and so on. The ultimate product was a complete record of how the students in the group achieved their task, how they overcame difficulties, what skills they developed, etc, and there was full ownership of the design and format by the student groups. Clearly, during this evolution the logbook had become a more factual product than an individual reflective journal, and it had less potential for emotional input than did a journal. I was aware that this change could have both positive and negative aspects, so I was interested in monitoring its effects.

To evaluate the impact of the final, electronic version of the project management logbook, I developed a questionnaire that provided qualitative evidence of its effectiveness as a means of supporting reflection on learning and as a tool that would enable students to consider the link between reflection on learning and continuous professional development. Reassuringly, with the exception of one or two students who from their responses were obviously not positively disposed towards working in a group, most students reported finding the logbook beneficial to them not just for group projects but also for working on an individual basis.

I am very fond of quoting the literature on students' ownership of their learning and on the goal of developing the autonomous independent learner. What was most interesting about this project from a learning point of view for me was that when it became time to change the rhetoric into reality, it proved time consuming, thought provoking and challenging.

I learnt a great deal about the real meaning of self-assessment, about the need to take risks where it is feasible to do so and about the value of giving students a sense of ownership of their learning. What is particularly pleasing about the outcome of the project is that positive feedback came from both staff and students involved in the programme. What is more, the Department of Architecture became convinced to introduce the format into one of their computer-based learning programmes. Students who were involved in maintaining a project management logbook alongside a design project recently won a prestigious prize in a competition sponsored by RIBA, the professional body for architects in the UK. The logbook was a key component for the decision makers in this competition.

It is worthwhile reflecting on the relationship of assessment to student learning, an issue that, at least at the outset, threatened to derail my efforts to introduce the journal/logbook to engineering students. There has always been a strong tendency towards acceptance of the view that students work to assessment and won't engage in learning that is not assessed. If we explore our own assessment strategies carefully, we can surely see that some of our strategies are artificial, with the emphasis being on summative assessment. It is often the case that students don't fully understand assessment criteria primarily because they are tutor derived and generally written in tutor-friendly terms. I believe that we need to do much more work to support our students in developing a shared understanding of assessment criteria and of the purposes of assessment – as well as a recognition of the potential value to learning of many activities that are not directly linked to summative assessment.

In the situation described in the case, we can ask why the new electronic format for presenting project outcomes appeared to influence the students' response so much. This new format was of course open to scrutiny by the project assessors, visiting industrial contacts and peers. Since students still tend to work in a competitive manner even at postgraduate level, the high visibility of student output may well have been a factor in the success of the shift. Interestingly, a similar response has been observed in other situations where there has been a shift to electronic presentation formats.

Was this change in format the main driving force in changing the students' attitudes? Or was it the fact that the concepts of 'reflection on learning', 'personal development planning' and 'continuous professional development' are becoming more mainstream and thus more acceptable to students? Or was it the granting to students of ownership over the definition of excellence within a particular learning context? I think it likely that a combination of factors resulted in the success of the initiative described and perhaps the lesson for us as teachers and facilitators of student learning is to take the risks associated with empowering our students to better prepare them for the demands of the ever-changing world of work.

It is difficult to ask teachers working within their own disciplines to engage in the level of development described in the case. However, by having such teachers work in partnership with educational developers, it is possible to effect major change at classroom level. The goal still remains, though, to encourage students to take responsibility for their own learning as a matter of course!

CHAPTER 6

THE REFLECTION JIGSAW

Case reporter: Helen Woodward

Issues raised

This case focuses on some of the difficulties that can arise during implementation of personally expressive and thoughtful assessment items such as portfolios and reflective journals.

Background

In the Faculty of Education and Languages at the University of Western Sydney, Australia, the yearly intake of teacher education students into the three-year Bachelor of Teaching programme is on average 160. Entrants are drawn from a large metropolitan area in general and in particular from the south west of Sydney, a high density, multicultural area where the majority of students are the first of their family to attend university. About 28 academic staff were involved in the development and implementation of the new programme that is the focus of the case.

PART 1

It was like putting together the pieces of a jigsaw puzzle – and assessment looked like being one of the most difficult pieces to fit. During the early 1990s, the Faculty of Education and Languages at the University of Western Sydney reviewed the Bachelor of Teaching and decided to implement a new programme over the following three years. The Faculty was already renowned for its innovative, forward thinking in the field of education and this new programme was to be no exception. However, as we tried to fit together the many aspects involved in creating the new programme, it reminded me of a jigsaw.

On the face of it, reviewing and rewriting a programme should not have been a problem, but as we gathered together a group of academic experts, innovators, external agencies and economic rationalists, the size of the puzzle began to dawn on us. The work proved to be frenzied, controversial and extremely difficult – and that was only the rewriting section! Implementation was another story altogether.

One of the highlights of the new programme was its final subject. It would be the only subject the students would study during their last semester. The subject that we developed (called the In-School Semester Practicum) was a 10-week school experience that contained five weeks of school involvement, during which the students participated in the 'life' of the school – observing, assisting, researching and preparing teaching strategies and programmes for their practicum class, and five weeks of teaching. In addition, the students were to carry out individual research projects based on their own learning needs and site-based projects that would utilize their expertise.

We felt that we had designed an innovative final subject. Now what could we devise in the way of assessment that would be both appropriate and as innovative as the course itself?

What assessment methods would you choose for the new course?
What methods do you think were actually developed?

PART 2

I was responsible for designing the assessment procedures for the final subject. I relied on my experience with portfolio assessment and my beliefs about individualized learning and assessment, and I thought it made good sense to implement a process that would start in year one of the programme and continue across the entire three years. The culmination during the final semester should be a vigorous, educationally sound assessment of the individualized learning of each student in the programme. Accordingly, I proposed a reflective journal and a portfolio.

First, the reflective journal. The team of staff working with me had experience with students using journals. In fact, the previous programme included journals in just about every subject – so many that the poor students were just about 'journalled out'. But while journals were rife, reflection was minimal. We recognized that the process of reflection needed to be taught and empha-sized, and, for consistency and integration, this reflection should be carried across the disciplines in one journal. The policy we developed was that there would be only one reflective journal across the whole programme. The format for the journal was to be introduced in the Teaching and Learning subject in the first semester. It would then be continued throughout the programme with end-of-semester summations to be filed along with the journal for future reference and for use in the portfolios.

In addition to the reflective journal was the portfolio itself. Again previous experience told us that simple collections of work, which constituted many 'would-be' portfolios, were of no benefit to anyone. Most such portfolios had little relevance to either learning or the learner and they were usually of such size that a set of wheels was necessary to transport them. Combining reflection with examples of work seemed to be one way to make the process more meaningful and to reduce the final product to manageable proportions. It made sense to begin the portfolios in first year, along with the reflective journals, and then to follow them up throughout the programme in order to ensure progression. My dilemma at this stage was how to make the portfolios relevant and how to give students an opportunity to demonstrate their learning.

As circumstance would have it, about that time I had the opportunity to hear Lee Shulman (of the Carnegie Foundation in the United States) speak one night at Sydney University. Several of his ideas set my mind racing. The State Government had just released a set of criteria for beginning teachers known as Desirable Attributes. I suddenly realized that this set could provide the criteria I was looking for. Lee also spoke about teachers demonstrating their learning to a panel. Aha! That's what I needed: a panel to assess the students' learning as evidenced by their portfolios – perhaps through an oral examination (viva). Some more pieces of the jigsaw puzzle were falling into place!

Eventually it was agreed that the criteria for the portfolio would be drawn from the Desirable Attributes for Beginning Teachers document and that a panel of four would conduct the final assessment of the portfolio at the end of the programme through a viva. The members of the assessing panel would be the student's mentoring academic, a representative from the school system, a second-year student and another member of staff. The big question was whether and how we would mark or grade the reflective journals, the portfolio and the viva.

My own thinking is that the diversity of learning that is displayed in a reflective journal or portfolio precludes using these instruments to compare students with each other. Therefore, I believe that journals should not attract marks but should be graded only pass or fail, as the learning is intrinsic to the process and different for each student. However, some of my colleagues did not share this belief. During a meeting held to discuss this issue, strong views emerged about assessment and about issues of control. For example, one colleague, Beth, commented, 'You are expecting me to spend time on an item (reflective journal) over which I have no control? – forget it.' 'Of course you can give marks for reflection and portfolios – you have to – otherwise the students won't do it', was Will's contribution. And Rosemary added, 'I don't have time to do what I want to do let alone do extra and for what? – no marks?' Because of my colleagues' reactions, it looked as though I would be unable to implement my grand plan. I was terribly disappointed. It was as though my almost complete jigsaw puzzle had broken apart and the pieces were all over the floor! What do I do now?

What do you think contributed to the reactions by the reporter's colleagues?
How do you think the situation might be retrieved?
What do you think actually happened?

PART 3

I decided to start with the reflective journals, as most staff would be involved with them at some point during the programme. Although staff had expressed great resistance to the process, all of them appeared to value reflection and the concept of journals. We sat down at a staff meeting and debated our differences. Rosemary claimed, 'I have my own form of journal that's different from the one prescribed and I can't see why I have to change to the one you've come up with.' Robert and Jen described how they established reflection in their subjects and how they used journals. The journals in their subject required students to report on their practice and tie it to theory. In Beth's subject, the students were required to read set material and reflect on it, while Will asked the students to read from a selection of articles and synthesize their understandings in line with their practical experiences. Recognizing that there was more than one way to reflect and more than one model to assist in this reflection, we reconsidered our previous position of mandating a single form of journal. Perhaps we could start off with the proposed model in the first semester as a demonstration of one way to establish reflection. Then, as the students experienced the variety of other methods used by teachers in their own subjects, the students would recognize a range of possibilities from which they could eventually choose one that suited them best. After this discussion, we identified the subjects that had journals as part of the students' work. We decided that we would use these reflective opportunities as the means of implementing our ideas concerning reflective journals across the whole programme. There would still be end-of-semester summations, encouraging the students to reflect on and synthesize their learning and thus link journals and reflections across the programme. This was not what I had originally envisaged, but at least we were moving forward and the puzzle was again taking shape.

The next piece of the puzzle to be put in place involved marks and grades for the journals. While I still believed that learning constructed during and because of reflection cannot and should not be given a mark, others had different thoughts on this matter. How was I to resolve this debate? After further discussion, I could see that there would not be progress if I maintained my initial position. It was finally agreed that the reflective journals in semesters one and six would not be given marks. They would be given only a pass or a fail grade. The journals in the subjects taught during the other semesters would attract marks as decided upon by the relevant academics, but the summations across the programme would not be graded in any way. It wasn't really a compromise – more all of us stepping back a little and considering others' views. I had to accept that my colleagues did not share my beliefs about grading journals, but at least we had fruitful discussion and could move forward in completing our jigsaw puzzle.

Implementing the portfolios and devising the framework for their assessment were the next steps we had to take. In order to prepare for the implementation of the portfolios, I ensured that I was on the teaching team for the first-year subject in which reflective journals and portfolios were introduced. I set the scene for the students and outlined the format for the journals. The first question the students asked was the obvious one: 'What does a portfolio look like?' Too bad I couldn't answer that! No one had ever done one so there were no examples and no history to put before the students. As a start, I decided to put my own portfolio together over the next few months. And what a 'mind blowing' experience it was! I hadn't realized what a learning experience it would be. It became obvious to me that, while the portfolios were to be based on Desirable Attributes for Beginning Teachers, there was another aspect that needed to be explored: the personal dimension. We needed to include a section that allowed the students to explain how and why they decided to become teachers. So the portfolio was finally taking shape and I had a basic model to show the students. From my own experience with a portfolio, I now had an absolute conviction about its value as a learning tool.

The viva process needed attention next. Through discussion with the staff who would be working with me in the final-semester subject, it was decided that as well as students 'showcasing' their learning through their portfolios, they would also have to use their portfolios in answering four preset questions. This would add another dimension to the assessment by requiring that students talk about their learning as well as write about it.

At this point we still needed one piece to complete our puzzle. How were we going to assess the portfolios? We couldn't give only a pass or fail grade as the portfolio represented such a large proportion of the final semester's subject, so what were we to do? We decided to take this question to the students themselves. On the first day of the semester, we opened the class with some discussion about marks and grades. This process continued until eventually focusing on the issue of grading the portfolios. After a lengthy but fruitful debate, the students decided that the portfolio as a document would be graded as pass or fail with strict criteria being set. These criteria would not regulate appearance or presentation but would be concerned solely with the quality of the content. At the same time, it was decided that the viva – to be known as the portfolio assessment – would be given a mark. A student would not be allowed to undertake the portfolio assessment unless she or he had obtained a pass for the portfolio as a document.

In 1993, we implemented the final stage of the programme and with it the portfolios and their assessment. To our immense relief, it all worked. The reflective journals had also made the journey relatively unscathed and so our jigsaw puzzle was finally complete. Standing back and looking at the final picture, yes, we could recognize it and we agreed that it looked good – but it was slightly different from what we had originally thought it would look like.

What other options might the team have tried?
What are the implications for future development within the programme?
What are the significant issues from this case for your own student assessments?

CASE REPORTER'S DISCUSSION

Effectively introducing reflective journals and portfolios across disciplines and over a three-year programme was challenging. The issues of ownership and perception of what students value were at the core of the case. Difficulties that arose in regard to the implementation of the reflective journals were compounded when the process, which was thought to be democratic, proved to be anything but. The design planning teams were not fully aware of the importance of ownership issues. Organizing and negotiating so that individual expertise and espoused theories can be considered requires careful planning and teamwork. Eventually we managed to negotiate the territory so that all those involved (including the case writer) were comfortable with the decision about the placement of reflective journals across the programme and the recognition and valuing of individual approaches. While the initial idea for one journal to be used across the programme was sound, it did not take into account the individuals involved. This lack of consideration deprived them of ownership of the subjects they were to teach. The question arises as to when and how to involve these faculty members.

The issue of marks and grades for the reflective journal also affected decisions about implementing and grading the portfolios. Faculty were of the opinion that students would not put effort into assessment items for a pass/fail grade. Some educationalists tend to support this notion, but I was hesitant about agreeing. I believed that giving a mark or grade to personally expressive and thoughtful assessment items such as reflective journals and portfolios changes the purpose, the learning and the reflection on that learning. The case demonstrates the process we went through in an attempt to resolve this issue. I am still uncertain whether this was the best resolution to the problem.

The perception that students would not want pass/fail grades was the stimulus for my going to the students themselves as a result of this debate. They supported my position and have been consistent in their views about grading of portfolios every year since. Negotiation with the students at the beginning also gives them a sense of ownership in the process. I'm not sure if their positive reaction is due to the way we present the issue or if it is for some other reason. We have just completed some research on students' perceptions of the portfolios that supports the contention that the approach we have taken promotes their feeling of ownership. Each year, however, we do get a small number (about 1 per cent) who comment in their subject evaluations that the portfolios are a lot of work for just a pass/fail grade.

Ownership is extremely important in this process, for both students and faculty. It is crucial that their ideas and opinions are considered. Just when and how this is done is a key issue when it comes to managing programme teams and when making decisions about assessment.

In the end, democratic team management is required if creative and worthwhile programmes are to be implemented. Support of those involved must be ongoing and differing viewpoints must be considered. It can be seen throughout the case that decisions were made sometimes democratically, sometimes not. It is difficult to predict how different the final picture would have been if we had taken another pathway or if the negotiation and recognition of ownership had been operationalized differently. Given the circumstances and personalities involved, it is unlikely to have been more positive than what we achieved.

CHAPTER 7

PORTFOLIOS FROM CYBERIA

Case reporters: Carol Bowie, Gordon Joughin, Peter Taylor, Brad Young and Craig Zimitat

Issues raised

This case focuses on issues related to the design and implementation of an assessment instrument appropriate for and congruent with the philosophy of a course in flexible learning.

Background

Early in 1999, three members of the Griffith Institute for Higher Education and two staff from Griffith Flexible Learning Services met to begin planning a Graduate Certificate in Flexible Learning for tertiary teachers to commence at Griffith University, Australia, in 2000. The Graduate Certificate was to foster the development of flexible teaching and learning practices of staff in universities and colleges and would consist of four subjects: Foundations of Flexible Learning, Designing for Flexible Learning, Implementing Flexible Learning, and a Project. During its first year, 15 participants were enrolled in the programme.

PART 1

We finished our meeting at 2.00 am! After months of discussion, planning, arguing, drafting and revising, we had completed the formal documentation required by the University Academic Board in a marathon effort to tie up all of the loose ends. We went home knowing that we now had a formal course submission, and that Griffith University's Graduate Certificate in Flexible Learning was on its way. During the planning process, we had gone through many of the stages of group development, including times of serious disagreement, difficulty in simply finding time to meet as a group, trying to accommodate a range of views that did not always appear to be compatible, and considerable variation in team members' experiences of teaching, educational backgrounds, and philosophies of learning and teaching.

Our formal documentation covered all of the University's requirements, including the need for the course, its aims and objectives, the content of the various subjects, how it would be taught, and the resources that would be required. In line with the theme of the Graduate Certificate (ie flexible learning), an important feature of the course was to be its use of networked learning supported by course- and subject-level Web sites. One issue that provoked some of the most intensive thought and discussion during planning was assessment. What method or methods could we employ that would be both appropriate for the content of the Graduate Certificate and consistent with its philosophy?

What assessment methods would you recommend for a graduate course such as this in flexible learning?
What methods do you think were actually adopted?

PART 2

The main assessment tool we designed was the 'online course portfolio'. We were happy enough with the concept of a 'portfolio' – the 'online' part of it was more problematic. Assessment by portfolio is commonly used in accreditation courses for tertiary teachers. The selection of materials for inclusion in a portfolio requires participants to become actively involved in the learning process, since they must use higher-level cognitive skills to analyse and evaluate their own work against set criteria to select the best package to present for assessment. We wanted a form of portfolio that could be dynamic and cumulative so that it could be easily modified, built upon and restructured over the course's life. Such a portfolio could continue to be a useful resource after graduation. We would provide some initial structure by specifying four core sections for each portfolio, namely evidence of having attained course objectives; reflections; a personal course plan; and a report on the final course project.

We realized, however, that portfolios could present some difficulties. Furthermore, we had spent many hours as a group considering how we could apply the portfolio approach across the course as a whole. We had exercised our brains even more in thinking about whether and how we could take advantage of the Internet to allow participants to create innovative portfolios that would be a unique expression of both the process and the outcomes of their learning. In our final analysis, we decided that there were several important issues and questions that we had to keep in mind as we used this innovative assessment tool for the first time.

What do you think are the main issues and problems to consider in implementing an 'online portfolio'?
What do you think happened when it was introduced?

PART 3

We recognized four important issues, which we identified for ourselves as a series of questions:

1. How would the 'portfolio' approach work in practice?
2. Would the portfolio used at the level of the whole *course* work across four different subjects and four subject convenors?
3. Would the online form of the portfolio – using the Internet – prove to be workable?
4. Could we successfully orient participants to the online course portfolio without intensive face-to-face contact with them?

We were very interested to see what would actually happen during the first run of the course starting in February 2000. This is what we found:

1.   We were aware that the portfolio approach would require skills in reflection and self-direction and that it would be a new form of assessment for most, if not all, of our participants. How would they respond? Would they have the autonomy and motivation required to throw themselves into the relatively demanding activity of developing a portfolio? Furthermore, some subjects had quite specific requirements. The subject Designing for Flexible Learning, for example, required participants to produce a design or plan for some teaching. How much scope would there be for participants to actively decide what would constitute evidence of attainment of objectives, when some of the evidence may not be open to negotiation?

During the first run of the online portfolio, we found that, while some participants thrived under the creative challenge of the portfolio, for others it was a source of anxiety. One participant, Jane, said: 'I felt I was floundering a bit earlier in the semester … I like to have clear, carved-in-stone instructions on the work I'm expected to carry out', while another noted that 'there was much confusion as to exactly what was required in the course'. For some, the more structured approach taken by Gordon as the convenor of the subject Designing for Flexible Learning led to a (not necessarily desirable) feeling of comfort. One participant said: 'The weekly activities format of Gordon's Designing subject is just the kind of "hand-holding" I need.'

2.   We were curious to see what would happen in our use of the portfolio at the level of the whole course rather than at the level of individual subjects. How could we maintain such an approach, while developing individual subjects according to our individual preferences, conceptions of teaching and of learning, and with the different perspectives that arose from our varying backgrounds and responsibilities?

During the first run of the Graduate Certificate course, two answers to this question emerged. First, it became apparent early in the course that participants were strongly wedded to thinking of a course as a number of disparate subjects rather than as an integrated whole. That meant it took some time and many discussions to clarify that the portfolio was operating at course level and subsumed the individual subjects. Second, if thinking at the course level was difficult for participants, it was equally hard for the course team. As the four subjects in the course were implemented, it became apparent that they lent themselves to the portfolio approach to different degrees. The portfolio found its strongest expression in Foundations of Flexible Learning, while in the Project, which requires participants to work within a provided framework, student choice and self-direction operate at a different level. Only a single item – the project report – is required as evidence of the achievement of subject objectives. The subjects that commenced the course – Foundations of Flexible Learning and Designing for Flexible Learning – were developed in tandem as complementary parts of the whole course. The final two subjects – Implementing Flexible Learning and the Project – operated more as independent units.

3.   We recognized early on that an online portfolio could take many forms. We considered two. First, a portfolio could be created by a student uploading a series of documents to a specific part of the course Web site created for this purpose, utilizing a pre-determined structure. Second, students could create their own Web sites and structure the portfolios to suit their personal requirements. The first option would have been simpler, easy to create and manage, while the second incurred considerable risks, since participants would need to use ftp (file transfer protocol), learn some basic HTML (HyperText Markup Language), and obtain passwords. However, we believed that the second approach provided more flexibility, student control and scope for creativity, so that is the option we chose.

What we observed during the first run was that, for some participants, the development of a Web site was a simple task – they were familiar with the process, since it was already part of their work, and they enjoyed applying this approach in the new context of their own learning. For others, however, the process was difficult and frustrating, leading to long and unfruitful hours in front of their computer, and/or long phone conversations and e-mail exchanges with the subject convenors as they tried to resolve issues of pass-words and access to the course server to upload their work. Stephanie's reaction, three weeks into the course, epitomizes the reactions of a number of participants at that stage:

> 'I think it is time to give up. After sitting glued for the past 18 hours to my chair, trying to catch up, I have found that either I am dumb or [you need to] make a sound course in HTML a prerequisite for the flexible learning course. For the past three hours – it is now past 2.00 am, and I am afraid it is not the first time that I go to sleep at 2.00 am just trying to get afloat in this course – I have tried to get one single file that contains a diagram (my framework diagram) over to my Web page and I cannot.'

However, Stephanie persevered, and by the end of the semester, she was feeling confident and had a strong sense of accomplishment. Here is her final word to one of the convenors following feedback on a major piece of work:

> 'You deserve the biggest hug ever. I am really moved. Thanks for the very, very nice feedback. My word, this fuels me for the next two subjects with pure rocket fuel. Sure I will at some stage get frustrated in both the project and implemen-tation, but now I know I can (and will) overcome any difficulty. I promise, I will do my very best. Thanks for this.'

Linda's reaction was typical of those who didn't experience problems. She was particularly enthusiastic about the Web site aspect of the course and made a number of very positive comments about it:

- 'Don't give up on the participants' Web-site work! I know it's tempting, given the problems that some people had, but I found it very interesting and useful.'
- 'Being able to look after my own Web site encouraged me to ensure that only good material… went up.'
- 'I was fortunate enough not to have any problems with my password or the technology, so I was able to take full advantage of the flexible nature of the subject.'

One of the anticipated benefits of the participants' Web sites was that the sites would allow the participants in the course easy access to their colleagues' work. Some participants found this facility extremely useful, others were neutral. We teachers had some difficulty, since we usually wanted to see how all participants had dealt with a particular issue. To do this, we needed to move from one point in one Web site, to a similar point in the other sites – with 15 participants, this movement represents a lot of clicks, and it is not possible to move quickly between participants' sites. Notwithstanding this, the ability to view participants' work on their Web sites whenever we wanted to and without recourse to print versions was certainly convenient.

4.   We knew that adequately introducing the participants to the unfamiliar medium of the online portfolio would be crucial to its success. And in light of some of the observations already recorded, we clearly need to do more. For the first run of the Graduate Certificate, we began the course with a half-day meeting with our participants. While we used some of the time to introduce ourselves and the requirements of the course, we also familiarized the participants with the technical requirements of the portfolio, including the nature of the Web sites they would be developing, the ways in which they could create and edit their sites, the ftp process, and password requirements. This introductory meeting was supplemented with technical instructions on the Web site as well as thorough descriptions of what we intended for the portfolios.

After our initial experiences, we are now acutely aware of the need to provide a longer, more comprehensive and more academically engaging orientation. All of the issues noted so far need to be addressed at some level at the very start of the course – our focus on technical matters at the beginning of this initial offering directed participants' attention away from the more important issues regarding the nature of the portfolio, the educational benefits of the portfolio being on line and the need for them to develop a whole-of-course approach.

How well do you think this development was handled?
What implications does the case have for your own assessment practices?

CASE REPORTERS' DISCUSSION

As a result of the first run of the course, we have come to a number of tentative conclusions about the online course portfolio. We have also planned several changes for the next offering. But we consider the online course portfolio to be a 'work-in-progress', so we still have unanswered questions at the core of our enterprise.

What have we learnt? These are some of our conclusions at the end of a difficult year.

We are confident that the online course portfolio can work well for many participants. A number of Web sites developed by our participants reflect, in their very structure, a significant progression in thought. As one put it, 'I have gone from feeling all the information I have learnt looked like this (picture of box overflowing with papers) to this (very well structured Web site in which the portfolio items are mapped against subject aims in a table, with links to the relevant items).' The Web sites also allow the peer review process to work easily, and the process is accessible to all.

These positive outcomes were highlighted on the faculty side by Carol's comment: 'I really was very happy at the end of the semester to have all of it visible online and I could easily see against our course objectives that participants had met the reflective practice [requirements of the course]. I could see over time their development. I could see where they had modified things and the quality of what they'd added to second and third drafts which gave me satisfaction that they'd done what I'd wanted over time.'

Other conclusions suggest points for us and others to keep in mind or ideas for improving the online portfolio:

- There must be a clearly defined purpose for the portfolio – as well as clear direction, clear aims, clear structure, and a coherent approach to developing it over the course.
- The portfolio will necessarily take different forms as participants move through the course's different subjects. Although this is a modification of our original intention, we are now comfortable with this realization, and while we see a need for some consistency in approach across subjects, this does not necessarily imply uniformity.
- For the participants' sake, we need to present an exemplar Web site – something we were unable to do first time around.
- Innovation is difficult for a team of staff who have not taught together previously. Developing cohesion takes time, patience and building up a store of common experiences and understandings. But the advantages to be gained by persevering make it well worth devoting the time and effort to working as a team.

Finally, the questions that remain for us would also need to be addressed by others seeking to adopt a similar practice:

- How can we best support students as they come to grips with what is required and with the innovative and unfamiliar form of online portfolio assessment?
- How can we best manage the anxieties that innovative assessment can give rise to?
- How do we help students maintain their focus on the academic aspects of their tasks and keep in perspective the technical hurdles they perceive?
- How can proprietary online learning environments (such as WebCT, First Class, Lotus Learning Space, and Blackboard) be used creatively for developing online course portfolios?
- What are the essential cognitive processes that students go through in creating their own portfolios and critiquing the portfolios of their colleagues?

- Are students *actually* going through the process we *think* they are as they develop their portfolios?
- How would participants compare the online course portfolio to other forms of assessment?
- What value is added to teaching and learning by the online nature of the portfolio assessment for students and staff?

CHAPTER 8

PORTFOLIO ASSESSMENT? YES, BUT...

Case reporters: David Baume and Mantz Yorke

Issues raised

This case focuses on the issue of optimizing reliability in the assessment of portfolios.

Background

The UK Open University (OU) is a large, distance-learning university. Established in 1970, it now has some 200,000 students (over 2,000,000 during its lifetime), 1,000 academic staff, 2,000 support staff, and 7,500 part-time tutors (called Associate Lecturers). Most full-time staff are based at Walton Hall in Milton Keynes. The University has 13 regional centres across the United Kingdom. The University's Centre for Higher Education Practice (CeHEP) was set up in 1997 to develop courses to train university teachers (as well as to conduct research on the training of university teachers and to run major national educational development projects).

The research described in the case was undertaken by the authors while Mantz Yorke was visiting professor in CeHEP. The 'we' in the case refers to the course team when describing course planning and operation, and to the authors when describing the research.

PART 1

We were in the process of analysing the first two sets of assessment results for The Open University's new course on teaching in higher education. What?! Only 60 per cent pass/fail agreement between assessors overall? After all the work we had put into planning our assessment, how could this be?

In developing an assessment strategy for the new course, we had faced these questions:

- How do you assess the capability of professionals, in this case professional lecturers who are also colleagues?
- How do you make that assessment valid, reliable, rigorous, fair, and possessing all the other virtues we'd hope for in a good assessment system?
- And, this being The Open University, how do you plan to do all this for hundreds or thousands of people at a time?

Our answer had been portfolios, with lots of effort applied at every stage of the teaching and assessment processes to maximize reliability.

Why portfolios? Three main reasons.

First, building a portfolio means assembling real evidence, in this case evidence of teaching ability, rather than writing essays or reports about teaching. It means the lecturer saying: 'Here is a picture of me, teaching and assessing students.' Portfolios can mean valid and authentic assessment.

Second, building a portfolio means being reflective and critical about the evidence and what it suggests. It means the lecturer saying: 'Here's what I think about my teaching. Here's why I teach the way I do. Here's why I think the teaching was good, or less good. Here's how I am improving it.' Portfolios require reflection.

Third, building a portfolio additionally means making an explicit claim about teaching ability. In the portfolio the lecturer says, in effect, 'Here's how this evidence and this reflection show that I have attained each of the course outcomes in turn.' This kind of portfolio involves self-assessment.

We also identified two minor reasons for using portfolios. What better way for teachers to learn about portfolio-based assessment for their students than to assemble, and be assessed on, their own portfolios? Also, a portfolio, unlike an exam script, can live and grow over time, recording continuing professional development as well as initial qualification.

The qualifications environment in which we developed the courses on teaching in higher education had a huge effect on the design of the courses and the assessment process. In 1992, the UK-based Staff and Educational Development Association (SEDA) launched a process to accredit the professional ability of those who teach in higher education. The SEDA Teacher

Accreditation Scheme 'recognized' programmes for training higher education teachers. To be recognized by SEDA, a programme must above all ensure that those who successfully complete it have met specified outcomes, and have done so in a way demonstrably underpinned by specified principles and values. In summary, the abilities required are to: plan teaching sessions; teach; assess student work; monitor and evaluate teaching; keep records of teaching; cope with the demands of the job; and reflect on practice and continue professional development. These abilities must demonstrably be underpinned by an understanding of how students learn; a concern for students' development; a commitment to scholarship; a commitment to work with and learn from colleagues; concern to ensure equality of opportunity; and continued reflection on professional practice.

In 1999, a new professional body, the Institute for Learning and Teaching (ILT), was set up in the United Kingdom for those who teach in higher education. The ILT accredits courses to train higher education teachers and admits into membership those who pass them, as well as allowing entry by direct application to ILT. The ILT specifies five main areas of work in which teachers must show their ability, underpinned by specified professional values and knowledge.

CeHEP developed a programme of three courses, each portfolio-based, accredited variously by SEDA and ILT. This case study concerns the first of these courses, on teaching in higher education, which leads to the SEDA Associate Teacher qualification, and in due course, it is hoped, also to ILT Associate Membership. The team designing the course was concerned to make assessment as valid and as reliable as possible. Some of the steps taken to achieve these two goals were adopted or adapted from normal OU practice; others were developed especially for the course.

The portfolio that each participant produces for the course on teaching in higher education is arranged in sections, one section for each of the seven course outcomes. Each section of the portfolio contains two main kinds of material: **evidence** and **claim**.

Evidence may include, for example, lesson plans, assessed student work, student feedback, or reports of observations of teaching. Most of this evidence will have been produced anyway during the teacher's work.

The **claim** is an explicit and reasoned assertion by the lecturer that the evidence shows that he or she has achieved each specified course outcome, and has done so in a way that is underpinned by the specified principles and values. The claims are specially written for the portfolio.

Detailed guidance is given on each step of writing the portfolio. Sample claims, with tutor comments, are also provided. We did not want the business of writing portfolios to get in the way of the lecturers thinking about, developing and showing their abilities as teachers. Participants receive detailed written feedback from their tutor on several draft sections of the portfolios.

We cannot assume that all course participants have access to a good library on teaching and learning in higher education, so we provide course materials. These materials are of two kinds: Practice Guides on the major topics in teaching and learning, and Reader Chapters that provide, with commentary, some of the key theory and evidence that underpins the practical guidance.

A very detailed framework for assessment of the portfolio is provided to participants. We want it to be absolutely clear what 'passing the course' means, in terms of abilities developed and demonstrated. A total of 75 assessment judgements are recorded for each portfolio. This detailed prescription is not an attempt to remove judgement from the assessment process; it is an attempt to make the basis on which the judgements are being made as explicit as we can. Each of the seven outcomes must be passed for the course as a whole to be passed. An outcome can be passed as long as there is no more than one marginal fail on one component of that outcome.

To match the detailed information given to participants about the portfolio and its assessment, we give extensive guidance and training to those who will be assessing the portfolios. This includes, in addition to the framework of assessment requirements, detailed instructions on how to assess the portfolios. (Copies of the instructions for assessors are also given to course participants, as we want assessment to be an open process.)

During preparation for each round of assessment, all assessors are given the same one or two current portfolios as samples to read and assess. The assessors then get together for a day, share their judgements, and strive to reach agreement. This process leads to further clarification of the assessment criteria and standards the assessors will use when undertaking real assessments over the next couple of weeks. Advice emerging from this coordination process is also fed forward to participants and assessors on the next presentation of the course.

During the actual assessment, each portfolio is assessed by two assessors – tutors on the course – who assess independently. If they agree, their recommendation goes forward to the assessment board. If the two assessors disagree whether a portfolio should pass, a third assessor, usually a member of the team who produced the course, moderates the assessment of the portfolio. This third assessor's judgement becomes the recommendation to the assessment board.

So – everything is done in accordance with good educational practice and in the best traditions of the OU. Assessment requirements and processes are specified in great detail, and given to everyone involved; assessors are carefully selected, trained and briefed; assessment judgements are coordinated. A recipe for success?

Well, up to a point! As we looked at the mountain of data generated during the assessment of the first batch of 53 portfolios, we were variously pleased and startled at some of what we found. The pass rate at the level of individual outcomes was 92 per cent. There was reasonable agreement between the two assessors on whether a given candidate had passed a given course outcome – 87 per cent agreement. However, there was a much lower degree of exact agreement on outcomes (we used a five-point scale for assessing outcomes) – only 39 per cent. And – the judgement of most import-ance to candidates – first and second assessors agreed on overall 'pass/fail' for only 60 per cent of the portfolios.

We were disappointed. So we took a hard look at what had happened. We asked ourselves some searching questions: Why, despite all our efforts, was the overall assessment reliability no higher? What could we do to improve the reliability of assessment of the portfolios, immediately and in the medium and longer terms?

What do you think might account for the lower than hoped-for level of inter-assessor reliability?
What steps would you recommend taking to improve the situation?
What do you think actually happened?

PART 2

We first tried to understand why the reliability of our assessment was lower than we had hoped. A trawl through the sparse literature on portfolio assessment showed a spectacular range of levels of agreement between first and second assessor, ranging from 19 to 100 per cent. However, some of these results described a single overall assessment judgement, others an assessment made up from several different elements. As is so often the case, comparison was difficult, but we derived some little cheer from being in the middle of a range of reported degrees of agreement, rather than near the bottom! Our interpretation of the literature did, however, highlight for us the tension between reliability and validity in optimizing our assessment.

This tension posed a real dilemma in planning our assessment scheme. We want assessment to be valid; that is, we want assessment to test that the outcomes have been achieved. We also want assessment to be reliable; that is, we want agreement between assessors. One way to boost reliability is to drive down the number of separate elements that must be passed. However, a valid scheme for professional assessment and accreditation will often require several distinct abilities to be demonstrated. For example, how would students feel knowing that their tutor was competent at planning lessons, at teaching, at record keeping and at reflecting on his or her practice, but not at assessment?

In trying to reconcile these conflicting pressures for reliability and for validity, we looked again at the set of outcomes we assess. We agreed that planning teaching sessions, teaching, assessing student work, and monitoring and evaluating teaching are vital and distinct outcomes. Keeping records of teaching, reflecting on practice and continuing professional development are also important, but perhaps they could be subsumed by or combined with the others. And coping with the demands of the job is tricky to assess convincingly, and so might be dropped. Thus we might consider reducing to four the number of separate outcomes that must be passed, subject of course to external accreditation requirements. This, of itself, should improve reliability.

The requirement that each outcome be underpinned by specified values has added complexity to the assessment. But the idea that teaching is a values-based as well as a skills-based activity is one we hold dear, and anyway is reflected in the national accreditation frameworks to which we are committed. We thought about how we might simplify assessment, and hence reduce the scope for inter-assessor disagreement, without losing the underpinning values. One suggestion was that we might require that candidates show how, say, at least two values of their choice from the list underpin their attainment of each outcome, and also how, say, each value underpins at least two of the outcomes. This would reduce the number of assessment judgements to be made while maintaining the importance given to both the outcomes and the values. Or we might ask for separate accounts, first of how each outcome is demonstrably achieved, and then of how each value demonstrably underpins practice.

Finally, we analysed the assessment data in more detail. We asked: 'Where is there the most disagreement between the two assessors?' We looked at disagreement on the assessment of the outcomes and of the underpinning professional values. We found a particularly high level of disagreement on the outcome 'reflection on practice'. Why? One reason was that this outcome is actually three separate outcomes. Course participants must show that they have 1) reflected on their work, 2) as a result, analysed the areas in which they need to develop further, and 3) on this basis planned their further professional development. In looking at individual portfolios and at assessors' comments, we saw that assessors were disagreeing in particular about how explicit the needs analysis was, and about what exactly constituted a development plan. We clarified advice to candidates and to assessors, and we hope for improvement in pass rate and in assessor agreement on this outcome.

We also found a high level of disagreement about the underpinning professional value 'commitment to equal opportunities'. Not surprising, perhaps – it is a highly contested concept. However, we had hoped for better. We have now clarified advice to course participants and tutors on this. We have also decided to give to course participants materials on equality of opportunity that were prepared for a later course in the series.

It is too early to tell whether our interventions will have the desired effects. We are hopeful that they will. At the same time, one heretical question has occurred to us. Need we be excessively worried if we can't increase inter-assessor reliability, and thus that more people will fail the course than we might wish? Is failure on this course all that serious?

Of course failure is disappointing, but what actually follows from a failure? On this course, what follows is that the course participant who is judged to have failed is invited to do further work on the outcome(s) he or she has failed to demonstrate, and to resubmit. Such candidates receive detailed written feedback on the ways in which their work on the failed outcomes was judged unsatisfactory. Resubmission rates, and success rates at resubmission, are high. So maybe all's well that ends well, for the teachers and later for their well-taught students!

What do you think of the conclusions that were reached and the ideas for increasing inter-assessor reliability?
What are the lessons from this case for your own assessment practice?

CASE REPORTERS' DISCUSSION

As already mentioned, our experience highlighted for us the tension between validity and reliability in assessment. Both are crucial elements, but we chose in this instance to focus on reliability. We claim that we could improve reliability by decreasing the number of separate elements to be judged by the assessors, where all have to be passed for completion of the course as a whole. A brief look at the relevant arithmetic, using our own course as an example, shows why this would be true.

Performance in our course is assessed on each of seven outcomes. Overall, we found that the level of agreement between the two assessors on whether or not each outcome had been passed was 87 per cent. Given that each and every outcome has to be passed for the course to be passed, how much agreement would we expect on whether a particular candidate had passed or not? The answer turns on how independent a lecturer's performance on each outcome might be from his or her performance on every other outcome.

There is a spectrum of possibilities here. At one end of this spectrum, teaching is seen as a single unitary ability. This view would lead us to expect very high correlations among a candidate's performances on all outcomes, and in turn would lead us to predict an overall pass/fail agreement between the two assessors of, again, something like 87 per cent. At the other end of the spectrum, perhaps each of the seven course outcomes describes a capability wholly independent of each of the others. If inter-assessor agreement is assumed to be 87 per cent for any outcome, then the chance that the assessors will agree on all seven outcomes, assuming that the agreements are randomly dispersed, is $(0.87)^7 = 38$ per cent. The approximately 60 per cent agreement that we found is between these extremes, suggesting that various skills of a teacher are somewhat, but far from wholly, interdependent.

This reasoning does not just apply to assessing portfolios. It applies to any situation with more than one element that must be assessed. The greater the number of separate parts of an assessment that must be passed for a course to be passed, the more are magnified the effects of any unreliability of assessment on the separate elements being assessed. Again taking our own course as the example, what might happen if, as we suggested, we reduced the number of outcomes that must be passed from seven to four? Assuming the same inter-assessor pass/fail agreement on each outcome (0.87), and again assuming performance on these outcomes to be independent, we might anticipate an overall pass/fail agreement of $(0.87)^4$ (~ 57 per cent). The chances of disagreement are thus lower with four outcomes than with seven. Furthermore, if there were a similar degree of alignment of pass/pass and fail/fail decisions as we had previously observed, we would predict a significantly higher percentage of agreement on course pass/fail than the 60 per cent we achieved with the seven outcomes.

As shown in the case, the added complexity of including values as well as outcomes might be approached in the same manner, ie reducing to a minimum the number of discrete items to be judged, all of which have to be passed. However, a further step can be the sort of analysis we undertook of those individual areas in which there was the greatest degree of disagreement between assessors. This led us to identify outcomes that actually comprised more components than we had thought, and values in which we should provide better information and guidance to candidates and/or assessors. More generally, this kind of detailed discrepancy analysis enables prioritization, on a rational basis, of the effort to be applied to improving assessment on courses. A similar identification of the outcomes or questions on which students score less well might tell where effort might usefully be applied to the materials or the teaching of a course.

Again, it is too early to know if the particular changes we made are going to be successful or not. However, the notion of continually monitoring, evaluating, reflecting on and attempting to improve both teaching and assessment is both something that is encouraged in our course materials and something we believe in and model ourselves. We do practice what we teach!

Acknowledgement

The production of an Open University course involves a large team of people. I (DB) am very grateful to colleagues in, particularly, the Centre for Higher Education Practice and The Open University's Institute of Educational Technology for all their work in producing the course analysed here, and to the tutors and course participants for their commitment and effort.

CHAPTER 9

'UNPACKING' PEER ASSESSMENT

Case reporter: Nancy Falchikov

Issues raised

This case study looks at problems encountered during implementation of peer assessment and the attempts made to solve them.

Background

Napier University, Edinburgh, is a new university recently developed from a Polytechnic, which itself was an amalgamation of a College of Science and Technology and a College of Commerce. Most of the students who took part in the peer assessments described in the case study were undergraduates studying biological sciences (a programme that also included some psychology), though, more recently, students of social sciences have also participated.

PART 1

I first introduced peer assessment into my teaching programme at Napier University in about 1985. I was inspired by what I had heard about the benefits of student self-assessment and the autonomy it afforded, so I designed my own scheme for both self- and peer assessment. The participants were first-year students of biological sciences, and their initial task was to assess their own, and later a peer's, psychology essay.

In preparation, teachers and students independently identified the criteria by which the essays were to be judged: teachers in a meeting designed for the purpose and students in a workshop preceding the writing process. Reassuringly, there was considerable agreement among the students about what they considered to be essential. Even more reassuringly, the students' list of criteria agreed with my own and was essentially identical to the teachers' list. The students' workshop concluded with a discussion of the relative importance of the criteria listed. After the workshop, I took away both lists and the information about relative importance of the various criteria and prepared a marking schedule using the students' own words to further encourage 'ownership' of the criteria. The following week, I distributed marking schedules and essay titles and the students were instructed to write their essays and self-assess them using the agreed criteria. They were told that they should be able to justify their marking.

At this point, the first hint of disquiet among the students surfaced. Caroline, a confident mature student, seemed less than happy and soon voiced her view: 'Marking isn't my job. It's yours.' I responded by explaining why I was requiring them to take part in assessment (they would benefit from the experience) and what I saw as my job (to aid student development and independent lifelong learning). I was soon supported by other students, some of whom seemed excited by the prospect. I stressed that teachers would, in any case, be marking the essays as well. Caroline listened and eventually agreed to give it a go.

The essays were written and self-assessed over the next few weeks and copies were made in preparation for marking by teachers and peers. During a tutorial, each student was given a copy of a peer's essay (minus name). The students were asked to assess the peer essays in the same way as before, using the same marking schedule they had used to assess their own work. Meanwhile, teachers involved with the course also marked the essays, again using the schedule.

I was keen to see how well the peer and teacher assessments would agree with each other. On analysing the data, I found that, in about two-thirds of cases, peer and teacher marks did not differ significantly. In the other cases, peer marks varied in both directions compared with the teacher's – but examples of peer over-marking tended to predominate. This was interesting and I felt it was worthy of further investigation. In follow-up tutorials, individuals met with the peers who had marked their essays and the pair were joined by the teacher for a three-way discussion during which a final mark was negotiated.

From my point of view, everything appeared to go rather smoothly, in that most students seemed able to defend their marking decisions, those who had under-marked themselves or a peer received a boost of confidence and those who had over-marked were given an insight into the reasons for the discrepancies between their marks and those of the teachers. Moreover, many students said how helpful the exercise had been in assisting them at the writing stage. I felt pleased with the whole experiment.

However, when I read the student evaluations of the exercise, I saw another aspect to the story. While much of the scheme had been given the thumbs-up, a vocal minority pointed to problems. One anonymous respondent asserted: 'Some criteria were weighted wrongly.' When I asked for more feedback and clarification during the next class, one of the students, Moira, said that she felt that too much emphasis had been placed on referencing – 'nobody else is as fussy as you are!' Another comment from the anonymous evaluation form claimed: 'The marking schedule wasn't comprehensive.' During class discussion, another student, Karen, pointed out: 'Originality or the writer's own ideas counted for nothing.' However, the most frequently stated critical comment went along the lines: 'Marking someone else's essay is hard, as the person may be annoyed if their assessment mark is lowered because of you.' I also learnt that some students had experienced embarrassment, while others admitted to being 'a bit generous' in an attempt to head off such feelings. This, of course, might account for the discrepancies I had found between some peer and teacher marks. Finally, Marie and James expressed the opinion that inexperienced peers might not be up to the job. Several others agreed.

Despite the apparent smoothness with which the exercise had run, there seemed to be several important issues beneath the surface that needed addressing. What could I do to deal with them?

What do you see as the important issues here?
How would you deal with the students' concerns about peer assessment?
What do you think happened next?

PART 2

I decided that there were three key issues to address:

1. I had to ensure that the marking scheme was appropriate to the task.
2. I had to tackle the problem of student reluctance to award marks (in particular, low marks) to their peers' work.
3. I had to find a way to boost students' confidence.

I thought I had already done enough to ensure that the criteria agreed by teachers and students were comprehensive and suitable for the task in hand, and that the students had taken ownership of them. Clearly, however, there was room for improvement. So the next time I asked a (different) group of students to assess their peers, I told them about the reactions of the first set of participants and stressed the need for care and thoroughness at this stage of the process. I also included an 'open' category on the marking schedule, which students could fill in as they wished.

Students' discomfort with awarding marks appeared to be a more challenging problem – until I realized that perhaps the grading aspect was not the most important part of the process. Maybe it wasn't necessary for students to give marks to their peers. Maybe more emphasis should be given to the provision of feedback. Certainly, the formative aspects of peer assessment are beneficial irrespective of the final grading. Thus, in future marking schedules, in addition to a list of the criteria agreed at the outset, I decided to require all peer assessors to identify at least one particularly good feature of the essay and to provide at least one piece of advice about how it might be improved.

At the same time, I knew that, in order to persuade my colleagues to adopt the practice of peer assessment, I would need to provide them with some evidence that students were up to the task. Also, it might be that students would take the task more seriously if marks were involved than if this were not the case. Therefore, in future, in cases where I felt that it was important to be able to compare teacher and peer marks, I tried to make students aware of the tendency to over-mark and to encourage them to be more realistic. I did this by adding a brief outline of the mark ranges for each degree classification to the marking schedule, together with information about the distribution of degree classifications achieved by final-year students the previous year. And I added the reminder: 'Be realistic!' to the marking schedule.

For my next trial of peer assessment, then, I gave more emphasis to preparation for the process, I included an open category (or two) in the marking schedule, and I required students to reflect on the product or process being evaluated and to supply feedback to their peers. For this trial, the participants were again studying biological sciences with a psychology component. This time, however, they were asked to assess an oral presentation rather than an essay. After each presentation, peers completed an assessment form and awarded an overall percentage mark. Before moving on to the next presentation, students gave oral feedback to the presenter, starting with the 'good' features of the presentation.

It was lovely to see nervous presenters hearing about what their peers rated as good about their work. Next, the class told presenters what they might do to improve their presentations. I was interested to see how the students coped with criticizing their peers' performance. It was not uncommon for students to 'soften the blow' by modifying their criticisms. For example, Susan said that Denise's presentation had included 'a *touch* too much information'. Similarly, others used terms like 'slightly' or 'a little'. Kay's criticism of Joanne's presentation was softened by the inclusion of an explanation: 'She tended to have a bit of difficulty getting the points across. This was largely due to nerves, however.' Sandy suggested why Donald's presentation (which was one of the last of the day) might have been difficult to follow, by shifting the responsibility for the lack of clarity from the presenter to the audience: 'It's generally hard to keep listening further down the line.'

While the steps I had taken certainly improved the feedback component of the peer assessment, difficulties with the marking aspect persisted (although to a lesser extent than in the previous trial). Once again, peers tended to over-mark rather than to under-mark compared with the teacher, but the mean extent of over-marking was only 5 per cent (and under-marking, 3 per cent).

There were also some differences between the feedback provided by students and that provided by teachers. Peer feedback tended to concentrate on practical issues associated with the preparation and delivery of the talk more frequently than did teacher feedback. Teachers *were* concerned with presentation issues, but they tended to emphasize understanding to a greater extent than did the students. It was as though students needed to address practical problems before they could begin to concern themselves with issues associated with the quality of learning. Finally, some students felt that it was a great pity that they had not had the feedback before they were graded on their performance.

By this stage, I thought I could detect a trend and I could see the direction I might take with developing peer assessment. It was time to take the next step.

What conclusions would you draw from the trials of peer assessment reported so far?
What would you do next?
What do you think actually happened next?

PART 3

It looked as though I might continue to experience difficulties as long as students were required to mark their peers, but the feedback element showed definite promise. I had even decided to call the process I was developing Peer Feedback Marking (PFM) to emphasize this aspect, and I believed it would be more beneficial to students than simple peer assessment would be.

I decided to address three further important issues at this stage:

1. the nature and quality of feedback provided by students to their peers;
2. whether students might benefit from having feedback *before* finally submitting a 'product' (such as an essay or a presentation); and
3. the extent to which peer feedback might be useful when given *during* the preparation phase.

The participants in my next trial (which involved written work) were again students of biological sciences. They were in their fourth (final) year. The exercise, which was derived from work by Kenneth Bruffee (1978), took place over an interval of eight weeks and consisted of the following five stages:

1. Criteria were agreed in the usual way and essay titles, reading lists and brief notes on essay writing were supplied.
2. Students completed first drafts of their essays in their own time during the four weeks following the first stage.
3. Non-evaluative peer review took place during a tutorial. Each draft essay was read by a peer who prepared a short description of the main points of each paragraph and of the whole paper.
4. Evaluative peer review took place the following week, also during tutorial time. Using the agreed criteria, a peer critiqued the draft, identifying strengths of the essay and supplying suggestions for improving it.
5. Each student submitted a reflective statement on her or his experiences as reviewer and receiver of feedback. This statement was handed in two weeks later, along with the completed essay, and contributed 20 per cent to the final coursework assessment mark.

So what happened? Well, for a few of the students, anticipation of the exercise had generated some anxiety. Others, however, said that the exercise was building on their previous experience of informal critiquing. The responses of two of the students were representative.

Shiona, who had experienced some doubts and fears before starting the exercise, was reassured after completing it. In her reflective statement, she said:

'1. There are many errors that you make when writing an essay, but it takes someone else to actually notice them.
'2. The input from someone else can only serve to help. Two heads really are better than one.
'3. The exercise spurs you on to write a good essay and not leave it until the last minute.'

Neil described a rather different reaction:

> 'The fact that a peer is going to read your essay and be invited to rip it to shreds makes demands upon you to take extra care. There is nothing worse than somebody quietly smirking to themselves at your expense, and an attempt to avoid this becomes a priority when writing the essay.'

Overall, a vast majority of the group rated the scheme useful. Students identified a variety of benefits, in addition to being able to modify the essay before final submission. They appreciated having the chance to agree on the criteria in advance and the opportunities for reflection the exercise afforded them.

To what extent did peers and teachers provide similar feedback this time? I again found many similarities between the two, but, this time, I also found that students provided more positive feedback than lecturers, and a greater number of prompts and suggestions.

Finally, to what extent did students act upon the advice they received? In their reflective statements, most students reported acting upon some peer advice. What is more, with very few exceptions, I rated the advice students received as potentially useful to them.

So far, my experience with peer assessment (in the form of Peer Feedback Marking) has been very positive. I am continuing to refine the process and to investigate the many tantalizing issues that my various trials of PFM have raised.

What do you see as the potential benefits and potential problems associated with peer assessment?
What lessons does this case hold for you in implementing peer assessment?

CASE REPORTER'S DISCUSSION

My experiences with peer assessment, and particularly students' reactions to it, point out the tension between the formative and summative aspects of assessment. (For more detail on the various trials, see Falchikov (1986, 1993, 1996). As teachers, we are expected to create a climate in which students feel at ease and are able to improve their learning, and, at the end of the day, to use the outcomes of that learning in order to grade the learners. This is not a comfortable situation to be in, as the students soon recognized. While the students appreciated the opportunity to see the work of their peers at 'close quarters' and they found the agreed criteria helpful for the creative process, they found the act of awarding a mark both practically difficult and personally uncomfortable. Thus they shied away from the grading aspect of peer assessment.

At the same time, there was no question about the students' positive perceptions of the formative benefits of peer assessment. My various trials of peer assessment confirmed this, while simultaneously raising a number of important issues and giving me an insight into students' views. For example, two students made comments that suggested that their view of education included dependence on the lecturer or an overemphasis on the acquisition of information. Helen reported:

> 'It may have proved useful if a lecturer had read your essay – even to give a few pointers without giving too much away. A provisional mark may also have showed the individual students if they had incorporated the right pieces of information in their essay.'

Anna also speculated on whether it would have been better if the criticism had been supplied by the lecturer but concluded: 'I understand that the purpose of the exercise was to extend your own critical techniques as well as aiding in peer assessment. Therefore, it would have defeated the purpose if the lecturer had taken this role.' I would like to think that participation in the exercise may have played some part in this move towards independence!

The exercises also highlighted the importance of giving and receiving positive feedback. Several students specifically mentioned how they had benefited from receiving praise for strengths in terms of boosted self-esteem that had enabled them to accept and act on 'negative' criticism without loss of confidence. However, identification of weaknesses and suggestions for improvement were also rated as essential by students whose feedback had been limited to identification of strengths. Thus, we should remember that a balance between 'positive' and 'negative' feedback is essential. It was particularly pleasing to find that, while similar to feedback provided by teachers, feedback from peers contained more positive comments and more suggestions and ideas than that from teachers. PFM seems to be a great help both in encouraging student autonomy and in filling the gaps that so often exist in the provision of useful and timely feedback by overworked teachers.

References

Bruffee, K A (1978) 'The Brooklyn Plan: attaining intellectual growth through peer-group tutoring', *Liberal Education*, **64**, pp 447–68

Falchikov, N (1986) 'Product comparisons and process benefits of collaborative self- and peer group assessments', *Assessment and Evaluation in Higher Education*, **11**, pp 146–66

Falchikov, N (1993) 'Group process analysis: self- and peer assessment of working together in a group', *Educational Technology and Training International*, **30**, pp 275–84

Falchikov, N (1996) 'Improving learning through critical peer feedback and reflection', *Higher Education Research and Development*, **19**, pp 214–8

INSTITUTION-WIDE ASSESSMENT PROGRAMMES: THE US PERSPECTIVE

CHAPTER 10

WADING THROUGH GLUE

Case reporter: Barbara D Wright

Issues raised

This case study addresses two major issues: the need for informed and attentive management of institution-wide assessment efforts; and the importance of keeping the focus on improvement of student learning outcomes as the primary purpose of assessment.

Background

The University that is at the centre of this case is located in the Southwest of the United States. With a broad range of prestigious graduate and professional programmes and a student body of over 24,000 it is the flagship university of the region. It is a top-tier research institution with a wide range of doctoral programmes, and faculty are constantly reminded by the administration that it is their research and publication that distinguishes the University from the more limited 'comprehensive' state institutions of higher education around them.

PART 1

Since the mid-1980s, US teaching institutions have been under pressure from state legislatures, accrediting agencies and others to engage in institution-wide assessment to document and improve educational effectiveness. In this context, assessment is separate and distinct, on the one hand, from testing within courses to determine students' grades; and on the other hand, from traditional programme evaluation for purposes of quality assurance or to justify changes in such inputs as budget, faculty or facilities. Rather it focuses on the major discipline or the programme and leads to improvements in curriculum or teaching at the department level. Institution-wide programmes such as general education, and institution-wide expectations for students such as information literacy or critical thinking or values development, may also be the subject of assessment efforts.

About a decade ago, the University jumped on the assessment bandwagon as one result of having redesigned its general education curriculum. One major change was that general education requirements would subsequently apply to all students in all the colleges and professional schools on campus. Previously, only students majoring in Liberal Arts and Sciences disciplines had faced a formal general education requirement. Members of the University Senate wondered out loud whether the new curriculum with the general education requirements would be any better than the old one. So along with the new curriculum, the Senate approved formation of an *ad hoc* University Assessment Committee to assess its effects. Eighteen months later, after formulating learning goals for general education and doing some research on the emerging post-secondary assessment movement, the University Assessment Committee was awarded a three-year $250,000 grant from the Fund for the Improvement of Post-secondary Education (FIPSE) to develop assessment instruments and determine the effectiveness of the new curriculum.

At about the same time, the state Department of Higher Education (DHE) introduced an assessment mandate and pointed to the University as a model for other public institutions in the state. Administrators basked in the glow of the FIPSE grant and the approval of the DHE but didn't get involved in the assessment effort itself. The President, who had been associated with Educational Testing Service for many years, couldn't understand why the project called for local instruments in an open-ended format; he shrugged at the foibles of faculty and went about fund-raising and other business. The Vice President for academic affairs was thrilled that his understaffed office wouldn't have to write the annual report to DHE – the University Assessment Committee could take care of that. The University Assessment Committee saw itself as a faculty initiative with its own budget and its own agenda, and that suited the Committee just fine.

Kate Sanford, a faculty member from the humanities who had written the successful FIPSE proposal, became the Director of the project to develop instruments and *de facto* chair of the University Assessment Committee. She was a bright, organized and articulate individual better known for her creativity and dedication to undergraduates than for her research. She enjoyed wide respect on campus, despite her lack of research credentials, in part because she was clearly capable, independent – and gutsy enough to take on risky new ventures like this assessment business.

The project called for developing instruments or 'activities' that students were to engage in as a way of demonstrating their achievement of learning goals in the five areas of the general education curriculum: literature and the arts, western and non-western civilizations, philosophy and ethics, social sciences and comparative analysis, and natural sciences. The instruments were to be administered annually to a random sample of entering first-year students and graduating seniors. Early results would establish a baseline for what students had learnt in the old curriculum. It was hoped that in later years results would show intellectual growth or 'value added' under the new curriculum. Kate set out to involve a wide range of faculty in the creation of the instruments and made a point of establishing highly interdisciplinary teams for each of the five areas. 'After all', she argued, 'this is general education. We can't have the specialists just talking to each other and going off the deep end.'

Despite initial scepticism, the mixed teams worked very well. Faculty enjoyed discussing educational questions with colleagues from the other end of campus with whom they never would have had contact otherwise. There were some early curricular benefits, too. The philosophers, for example, began to revise their ethics courses as a result of discussion with Nursing and Business faculty, and the scientists were inspired to rethink their goals for introductory science courses after working with humanists and social scientists. It helped that faculty received hefty stipends for their participation, thanks to the FIPSE grant. It was perfectly clear to all of them that this was not the kind of research-oriented activity for which they could ever expect a merit award, much less promotion or other recognition.

By the end of the academic year, Kate had some excellent instruments in hand to administer to students coming for summer orientation. Nearly 50 faculty had participated on the five teams, and another 100 or so from all the colleges and schools on campus had reviewed the instruments before they were administered. The review process strengthened the instruments, but it also had indirect benefits: it raised consciousness across campus about the goals of general education, gave the assessment project greater visibility, underscored the importance of undergraduate education and created real suspense about what the results would be.

Most innovative was the activity produced by the western and non-western civilizations team, led by anthropologist Jack Beede. To avoid focusing the non-western activity on a particular region and thereby giving an unfair advantage to those students who happened to have taken their course in non-western civilizations on that part of the world, the team invented a fictitious island nation named Calteria. They created a history for the country, beginning with aboriginal inhabitants, who were then invaded by a seafaring people. They in turn were conquered and colonized by Europeans in the 18th century, then won independence in the mid-20th century. The team also created maps of Calteria showing physical features, rainfall, land use, mineral deposits and population density. As students progressed through the activity, they received new information about Calteria and were asked to answer questions about things like the country's probable social structure, religious practices, art forms and political or economic problems at different points in Calterian history. At the very end, students were asked to comment briefly on what it was like to go through this activity.

The instrument was administered to entering students that summer and to graduating seniors the following fall. The results were a crashing disappointment. Although seniors managed to score a little better than new students, few from either group did well on the activity, which required them to formulate their own answers in sentences or short paragraphs rather than select from a multiple-choice list. While the results could be dismissed for incoming students, they were more troubling in the case of graduating seniors. Most disturbing of all, however, were the responses to the final question. Time after time, seniors wrote that the activity was incredibly interesting, but 'nothing I ever took here prepared me to take this test' – or words to that effect. Kate was well aware that on this first run, the seniors were providing only baseline data – but at least those in Liberal Arts and Sciences should have learnt *something* relevant. Never mind the future use of the assessment instrument. What was going on *now*? Was it the teaching that was at fault? the learning? the assessment tool? some combination of them? Kate wondered what to do next.

What do you think are the issues here?
What do you think are the strengths and weaknesses of the assessment effort so far?
What would you recommend doing next?
What do you think actually happened?

PART 2

Kate was firmly convinced that assessment projects had to focus on *using* the evidence gathered during the project to improve student learning – and not get hung up on instrumentation, duelling statistical analyses or finger-pointing.

As for the findings from the non-western civilization assessment, Kate decided that what was needed next was a series of seminars with faculty from the departments that offered relevant courses. Together, they would talk about how to teach 'larger concepts' along with the detailed content that each faculty member was committed to covering in his or her particular course. They would revise course goals, rewrite syllabi, maybe bring in an expert to talk about the difference between 'deep' and 'surface' approaches to learning, and then re-administer the instruments to see whether their changes made a difference. She had just begun to organize the seminars when she was offered an attractive job as dean of the faculty and director of assessment at another institution. She left the University at the end of the semester.

As Kate departed, so did the whole approach to assessment that she had nurtured. Cliff Tarentino, an energetic professor from Communications, became the new chair of the University Assessment Committee. Cliff had a long publication list and an outspoken commitment to research. Under his leadership, the Committee reasoned that since the University was a research institution, 'research' was the appropriate metaphor for conceptualizing and carrying out assessment on campus. Consequently, the Committee adopted the practice of posing 'research questions', designing 'experiments', analysing the results of 'treatment' and reporting them to various units on campus, much as one reports research findings in a refereed journal article. Kate's plans for a seminar with non-western civilizations faculty fell through the cracks. So did the idea of yearly administration of the instruments that had been developed through the FIPSE grant. Cliff argued there were enough data from the first round to keep them busy for years.

Instead, in the final year of the grant, the 'research' approach was used to study students' general education course-taking patterns and the strengths and weaknesses in general education learning in different majors. The next year, the Committee surveyed alumni and alumnae on their general education experience at the University. After each study, reports were sent off to the relevant schools and departments, along with lists of recommendations and exhortations to make the necessary changes in order to improve students' outcomes and educational experiences. Little actually happened as a result of these reports, but the Committee was not overly concerned. 'Hell, we're holding up our end', Cliff asserted when challenged by someone who remembered the early days of the assessment project. The three faculty left on the Committee, all social scientists, were pleased that they could present their work on assessment as part of their research agenda, both for merit review and at professional conferences.

About three years ago, the University began preparing the self-study for its decennial reaccreditation. The new vice president for academic affairs – now 'provost' – approached the University Assessment Committee. 'You know', he said, 'accreditation really is a form of assessment, and our regional accreditor is looking for assessment results as part of our self-study, so why don't you guys lead our self-study?' Cliff agreed, and the University Assessment Committee morphed itself into the Self-Study Taskforce. Over the next two years, the self-study was written, the visiting team hosted, and reaccreditation confirmed. By that time, the original assessment project was but a dim memory. Cliff left the University to become chair of a communication sciences department at a prestigious east-coast university. The University Assessment Committee never did get reconstituted.

Meanwhile, campus life goes on. There's talk of redesigning the programme review process, which has been pretty haphazard till now. The strategic plan calls for strengthening the undergraduate experience and giving students more opportunities to participate in faculty research. An elite undergraduate honours college is being discussed, and student affairs is trying to get faculty to collaborate in creating more connections between curricular and co-curricular life. There's a vague sense that students don't spend enough time studying, but nobody knows how much time they really do spend, or what they do with themselves when they're not (although there are plenty of theories).

In response to general dissatisfaction with undergraduate education, the Board of Trustees has approved the creation of a new position, Vice Provost for Undergraduate Education and Instruction, and a seasoned administrator, Clarissa Hammermacher, has just been hired. She's from Missouri – a state where efforts to improve education through assessment have been quite successful. The Provost has charged her to 'create some coherence in undergraduate education and make it a priority', but beyond that he's given her a free hand. She has the feeling he isn't really interested in undergraduate education and would just as soon think about other things. Hammermacher believes assessment could be the key, but she hardly knows where to begin. If she (re)introduces assessment, will it end up a case of '*déjà vu*'?

What do you think of the outcome?
How might a rededication to assessment be accomplished at the University?
What are the implications of this case for successful management of institution-wide assessment initiatives?

CASE REPORTER'S DISCUSSION

'Assessment' in the US sense means looking at educational processes and trying to figure out on the basis of evidence (not fads, not intuition, not somebody's pet theory) what's happening and – most important – how outcomes can be improved. Assessment may use evidence gathered in individual courses, but it generally asks larger questions about what coursework and other experiences on campus add up to. For example, assessment may ask 'What are the strengths and weaknesses of our chemistry major?' or 'What does our Catholic tradition mean for our students' development? Do they really acquire the ethical and spiritual values we claim for them in our literature?' In this sense, assessment is not very different from total quality management (TQM) or continuous quality improvement (CQI) as they have been practised in business settings and in some service sectors. The general approach can be applied to virtually anything, from the clearly academic (eg 'Just how well is our writing programme working, anyway?') to student affairs and business operations (eg 'How efficient are our financial services?' 'What is the level of student satisfaction with co-curricular offerings?' 'How on-target are our planning and budgeting?'). Since the most fundamental aspect of an academic operation is education, however, the most frequent and serious application of assessment is to the major disciplines or programmes, professional training, and such core outcomes as communication and problem-solving skills, information literacy and the ability to work in teams.

In large institutions, which cannot afford the time and energy required to provide individualized feedback to each student, good assessment practice may call for assessing a sample of students and making changes at the programme level, on the assumption that everyone who goes through the programme will then benefit. Or institutions may use assessment to look at what the education they offer adds up to at an even higher level of aggregation, ie the whole institution. In that case, they are trying to understand, for example, what the student's major, plus general education, plus electives, plus living in a culturally diverse dormitory, plus maybe the university's emphasis on religion or on a particular ethical or intellectual tradition adds up to. The central concern in all this, even if it's at a couple of removes from the individual student, is always with learning outcomes, the quality of the educational experience, and how to improve it.

The case study rests on just such an effort to understand and strengthen an educational programme – general education – but it is also riddled with other issues: misunderstandings, missteps, distractions, personnel changes, competing agendas, counterproductive reward systems, ignorance, inattention and the like. These are the sorts of seemingly peripheral but powerful factors that, on virtually every campus in the United States, can get in the way of people being able to just sit down around a table and get to work examining and improving student outcomes. In other words, the business of assessment is not just an interesting and useful academic activity; it's a very political one as well, fraught with managerial and budgetary and territorial and other kinds of considerations. In the United States, at least, administrators or faculty wanting to do assessment ignore that context at their peril.

At the University in the case, the assessment project gets off to a seemingly good start, but the lack of administrative interest or financial commitment to the project is problematic. Time passes, and the project produces an interesting finding: apparently, the courses that contribute to the non-western civilizations requirement are out of alignment with the requirement's general education goals. Exploring what that means, and what should be done about it, could be a valuable undertaking. But that never happens. Instead, the statistical results (minus student comments) are merely reported to the campus at large, in the style of research articles, where the onus is then on others to respond. No seminars are organized, no conversations take place, nothing happens and nothing changes. The pattern repeats itself with the assessment committee's subsequent studies.

In the assessment effort described, the questions about student learning go to the heart of undergraduate education, the process is good, the instruments are excellent and the potential for them to yield information for improvement is great. That's not where the problem lies. The main problems are misunderstanding of what assessment is and how it should be done, inattention and/or ignorance on the part of administration, a reward system that undermines the whole assessment effort, and so on. In other words, the problem is not the assessment project itself; the problem is the context in which assessment is carried out. That context is traditional academic culture, at least as it prevails in the United States, with its enormous inertia and ability eventually to crush countervailing efforts.

It is often said in US assessment circles that the biggest challenge assessment poses is to the traditional culture of colleges and universities. Assessment demands a shift from defining institutional quality in terms of reputation and resources to defining quality in terms of educational outcomes. It requires a 'new paradigm' (Barr and Tagg, 1995): a shift from a focus on teaching – and the assumption that learning is strictly the student's responsibility or problem – to a focus on shared responsibility for learning. It requires, in some institutions at least, a re-evaluation of the proper balance between teaching and research, while at the same time offering new opportunities to create a scholarship of teaching and learning within the disciplines (Boyer, 1990; Hutchings and Shulman, 1999). Not least, assessment challenges a tradition of faculty autonomy that all too often has become counterproductive isolation, self-interest and defensiveness. It challenges a more recent but equally lamentable trend among post-secondary administrators to distance themselves from faculty and think of themselves more as the leaders of multimillion-dollar business enterprises than as educators.

The current academic culture in the United States is extraordinarily resilient. The case shows how even a well-funded, well-designed, initially promising assessment effort can founder as traditional campus values, established reward systems, administrative priorities, and behavioural habits reassert themselves. In the case, the assessment project galvanizes faculty, creates mechanisms for interdisciplinary communication and stimulates questions about how to improve the quality of undergraduate education. But just as participating faculty are on the verge of probing more deeply into questions of student learning, the project loses its focus and momentum and ends up offending against most of the principles of good practice in assessment (American Association for Higher Education, 1992).

What are the antidotes, if campuses are to reap the benefits of assessment? To change a campus culture requires knowledge, engagement and vigilance on the part of administrators as well as faculty. It requires a willingness to talk and work together on the part of many campus constituencies – constituencies that in many cases have not been in the habit of collaborating. For administrators, it means enlightened support for assessment efforts; responsiveness to the input of faculty, professional staff and students; informed, sustained attention over time; insistence that findings be used for improvement; connecting findings to planning and budgeting; and above all willingness to provide meaningful rewards for work well done. For faculty, it means assuming front-line responsibility for improvement of teaching and learning, candour and integrity in the examination of problems, and a rediscovery of productive collegiality in place of a rigid notion of faculty autonomy.

Finally, and on a more specific and personal level, it is worth considering Kate's role in the case. Was it just 'bad luck' that she moved on? What might have happened had she stayed with the project and persevered with her approach? I believe that, far from being 'bad luck', her departure was virtually unavoidable. Given her lack of administrative power or of status in research, she was in an environment in which she could be effective for a while, but not long-term. Without fundamental changes in the value system and reward structure of the institution, it was just a matter of time before she would be ground down. If she had hung on long enough, *perhaps* she could have initiated those fundamental changes through the assessment project, but only with the backing of administrative and faculty allies who had the kind of clout she lacked. And it's not at all clear where such allies would have come from. Kate recognized all this, and when an offer came from an institution that was more compatible with her idea of a quality undergraduate education, she went for it. Similarly, from an administrative point of view, it was not 'bad luck' that Kate moved on. Rather it was terrible administrative judgement. She was effective and should have been rewarded and supported for the job she did. She was a great resource, and they never noticed – again highlighting the crucial role of enlightened leadership in promoting and maintaining educational initiatives that are as important, but at the same time as demanding, as the assessment project described in the case.

References

American Association for Higher Education (1992) *Principles of Good Practice in Assessing Student Learning* (Assessment Forum), American Association for Higher Education, Washington

Barr, R B and Tagg, J (1995) 'From teaching to learning: a new paradigm for undergraduate education', *Change*, **27** (6), pp 13–25

Boyer, E L (1990) *Scholarship Reconsidered: Priorities of the Professoriate*, Carnegie Foundation for the Advancement of Teaching, Princeton, NJ

Hutchings, P and Shulman, L (1999) 'The scholarship of teaching: new elaborations, new developments', *Change*, **31** (5), pp 11–15

CHAPTER 11

Barking at Straw Dogma

Case reporters: Trudy W Banta and Sharon J Hamilton

Issues raised

This case deals with what happens when a university is confronted with the need to document its methods of teaching and assessing general education outcomes for students as part of preparation for a visit by its regional accrediting association.

Background

The US university that is the focus of this case is an urban commuter campus with some 25,000 students studying in 18 colleges (academic units) that have proud histories of functioning autonomously. Professional schools of medicine, nursing, dentistry, law, engineering, social work, education, business, and public and environmental affairs predominate, but there are also strong schools of liberal arts, science, and the arts.

PART 1

In 1989, our university's Vice President for academic affairs appointed a committee to develop a new campus-wide approach to 'general education' – ie the generic knowledge and skills that form the basis of a liberal education and the foundation for disciplinary specialization. This committee made recommendations for a set of general education principles that appeared to be sufficiently broad to encompass the concepts of general education espoused by faculty in most of the disciplines represented at the university.

Nevertheless, some faculty objected to some of the principles, so they were not approved by the university-wide Faculty Senate.

In 1992, the visiting team sent by the regional accrediting association made this observation about general education at the university: 'We note the absence of a sound and coherent experience in general education that is monitored at the campus level.' Moreover, the team pronounced assessment at the university 'widely dispersed and uneven'. The team directed the institution to develop a campus-wide understanding of general education and appropriate methods for assessing generic student outcomes.

Between 1989 and 1998 several groups were formed to advance general education at the university. Each produced a report, then was dissolved, only to be replaced by another group. Finally, in 1998, a compromise set of six Principles of Undergraduate Learning (PULs) was adopted by the Faculty Senate. The PULs were generic and loosely constructed so as to appeal to the widest possible range of disciplines. They included: communication and quantitative skills; critical thinking; integration and application of knowledge; intellectual depth, breadth, and adaptiveness; understanding society and culture; and values and ethics. Each of the university's 18 colleges was asked to implement the Principles within its own discipline and to assess student learning in whatever ways faculty deemed appropriate. Thus 'critical thinking', for example, might be defined, taught, and assessed differently in nursing, economics and biology.

During 2000, the campus began to prepare for the decennial visit of the regional accrediting association in 2002. High on the list of issues to be addressed in the required self-study was the need to document the methods for teaching and assessing student learning outcomes in general education, as had been mandated in 1992. Since each college had been asked simply to implement and assess the Principles in its own way, and no central authority had been checking to see how this was progressing, the obvious (but potentially thorny) question arose: 'How should we go about assembling the documentation we need in this area?'

Given the manner in which the PULs had been promulgated and implemented, what steps would you recommend taking to gather the required information in a coherent fashion?
What methods do you think were actually used?
What do you think happened?

PART 2

Since the PULs had been disseminated to the colleges for each to implement and assess in the way it wished, it seemed only natural first to approach the colleges and request reports that would document instruction and assessment in general education – these then to be collated to produce an overall report for the university. Big mistake! The responses were frequently anything but helpful. Three examples can give an impression of the flavour of the reactions:

1. The chair of the Department of Economics conducted his own analysis of a document prepared by the regional accreditor that was intended to be helpful to faculty considering assessment, by characterizing beginning (Level 1), intermediate (Level 2) and advanced (Level 3) levels of assessment implementation. He wrote:

   'In the Jewish liturgy there is a prayer, Ve'ahavta, specifying actions that show the congregant's commitment to Judaism. Part of it says: "You shall love the Lord your God with all your mind, with all your strength and all your being. Set these words, which I command you this day, upon your heart. Teach them faithfully to your children: speak of them in your home and on your way, when you lie down and when you rise up."

   'The accrediting agency's questionnaire on assessment seeks a similar level of commitment. Instead of rating a department on how it assesses students and the impact of that assessment process, it asks about faculty belief and public espousal. For example, to reach Level 2 in the category of institutional culture a department must value the assessment of students and have a statement of purpose that specifically mentions the importance it attributes to assessing learning. Level 3 requires that assessment become a department's "way of life". To reach Level 3 under institutional support, it is the department chair's responsibility to see that the faculty increasingly talk about assessment to each other, to students and administrators, and to anyone else who might listen to them!

   'These requirements are nonsensical. If I told my students in economics that I would grade them on how often they spoke about economics at home and among their friends and whether they truly believed in the power and elegance of economic analysis, they would probably kill me. Why should the faculty be graded on attitude and obeisance? Presumably it is the duty of the faculty to question the efficacy of new programmes. Only a religious dogma would be exempt from such scrutiny.

   'I have no objection to describing what my department does to assess student learning but I will not rate their degree of belief. I certainly would not downgrade my colleagues for questioning the efficacy of a programme. I think our college should simply refuse to complete this survey and explain why it is so objectionable.'

2. Another faculty member in the liberal arts opined: 'The six Principles of Undergraduate Learning might not have been approved by the Faculty Senate in 1998 if faculty had known that they would be called upon subsequently to provide evidence that they were teaching the PULs and assessing students' achievement of the knowledge and skills identified in the Principles document.'

3. Three faculty in administrative positions had proposed an electronic port-folio for first- and second-year students as a means of 1) focusing faculty and student attention on the PULs during introductory courses and 2) assessing student knowledge and skills as described in the PULs. An inter-disciplinary group of faculty were appointed to a committee to oversee the development of the portfolio.

As long as the student was viewed as the portfolio developer, selecting examples of work accomplished within courses and outside (eg in extra-curricular activities or off-campus jobs or volunteer work) to illustrate his or her achievement of the PULs, faculty on the committee were supportive. But then the subject of quality of the portfolio materials surfaced. The prospect of faculty-assigned grades and written comments appearing on the student work selected for the portfolio provoked comments about the invasion of faculty privacy and abridgement of academic freedom. The notion of viewing multiple student portfolios across a single course or across an entire curriculum was criticized. One senior faculty member artic-ulated faculty feelings in her statement, 'I feel uncomfortable having my grading processes available for scrutiny by the general public. What goes on between me and my students is a private, academic matter.'

One alternative for gathering information about the implementation and assessment of the PULs across academic units was attempted early in the accreditation self-study process. The position of Faculty Associate for Undergraduate Learning was created, and three respected faculty members were selected as Faculty Associates. Each was assigned two of the PULs and asked to document the experience of implementing those principles and assessing student learning of the specified knowledge and skills in each of the academic units offering undergraduate courses. The Faculty Associates decided to conduct a series of joint interviews with associate deans for under-graduate learning and with selected faculty in each school.

They were genuinely astonished at the range of responses to assessing general education that they unearthed, and dismayed by the behaviour of some of their colleagues. One associate dean folded his arms, looked down at the floor, and muttered: 'I don't even know why I have to waste my time here. It's all in the written report I filed last spring!' They discovered academic units that suggested – but did not require ('because it would interfere with academic freedom', according to one associate dean) – that the PULs merely be listed in each course syllabus. Other academic units, while more compliant with the requirement to include the PULs in every syllabus, listed them but devoted no explicit attention to them in assignments or grading, and made no attempt to explain how they were integrated into coursework. 'Our faculty are already too busy just covering the work of the course. We've no time to add on the PULs!' Although this was the comment of one associate dean, it was indicative of the comments of many others.

Many of the professional schools could not articulate what they expected in terms of specific skills or knowledge from general education prerequisites in their academic programmes. 'We've just always required this course', was the usual response, accompanied by a shrug of the shoulders.

The Faculty Associates were frustrated and dismayed, almost to the point of giving up. 'Our colleagues are so resistant to the notion of these PULs. Our task is impossible!', they lamented.

How would you respond to the various reactions by faculty to the request for documentation of the implementation and assessment of the PULs?
What would be your next step in developing this component of the accreditation self-study?
What do you think actually happened next?

PART 3

Despite apparent faculty resistance, university administrators pressed ahead on two fronts: the development of electronic student portfolios and the collection of campus-wide information about the PULs.

During the fall semester of 2000, three faculty members agreed to pilot one section each of the electronic student portfolio, wherein students would upload evidence of their work with each of the PULs during their first semester at the university. Concurrently, the Faculty Associates applied their strengths as academic researchers to the task confronting them. The anthropology professor in the group began looking at faculty resistance as a cultural phenomenon and used ethnographic research methods to build his collection of evidence. The Associate from the School of Social Work took a sociological perspective, valuing the different cultures of each academic unit and looking for materials and evidence within those different cultures. The Associate from engineering used pragmatic methods of data collection to build his corpus of evidence. They assiduously sought the information they needed to prepare a matrix summarizing how each academic unit was assessing the PULs. This was to be presented to the campus-wide Assessment Committee.

Near the end of the semester, the interdisciplinary committee charged with overseeing the development of the portfolio was convened to observe what students had achieved. 'This is wonderful!', exclaimed the faculty representative who previously had expressed concern about privacy. 'So often I am asked by departments that list our course as a prerequisite to demonstrate that students really have achieved the required skills. These portfolios have the capacity to show every student's level of proficiency. That will really reduce the amount of time I need to respond to faculty questions.' While not all the concerns of the faculty were assuaged during this meeting, the focus was on issues of *student security*, rather than *faculty insecurity*.

Similarly, near the end of the semester, the Faculty Associates presented their matrices on assessment of the PULs to the Assessment Committee. These matrices showed, for each academic unit, where and how the PULs were taught, how they were assessed, and how the assessment information was used. Information garnered from school annual reports, from interviews with faculty and associate deans, and from other materials ensured that each unit was well represented on its matrix. At the same time, it was clearly evident that much work still needed to be done to properly assess general education (the PULs) across the campus.

During the meeting, the first responses came from the most resistant college, arts and sciences: 'We don't have time to do assessment of the PULs in addition to teaching our courses', barked one associate dean, echoing one of the comments we recorded in Part 2. Then came a surprise. 'But look at the matrix. It's not in addition to − it's all integrated with the work of the courses', said the associate dean from one of the professional units. And the conversation took a turn that we could not have scripted better ourselves. Faculty started focusing on the role that the PULs played in enhancing student learning within their disciplines and professional education, and how providing the information for annual assessment reports and for the Faculty Associates had strengthened their understanding of the importance of assessment for improving student learning.

As the meeting progressed, the members of the Committee became increasingly aware not only of the task at hand, but of how much work had been done for them by the Faculty Associates. The criticisms expressed at the beginning of the meeting, which had threatened a stormy encounter, became transformed into murmurs of acknowledgement, then comments of appreciation, and finally, and most surprisingly, a spontaneous burst of applause for the work of the Faculty Associates.

What do you think accounted for the changed reactions by the groups looking at the electronic portfolios and the matrices?
What are some implications of this case for engaging your own faculty in assessment activities?

CASE REPORTERS' DISCUSSION

Reaffirming as the two expressions of understanding mentioned above were at the time, we know more than to accept them as indicators of a general transformation. What we need to do now is draw upon what we have learnt over the past two years and use these lessons to try to bring more faculty to the level of awareness demonstrated in these two late-semester meetings. We have drawn two important conclusions from our experience:

1. The transformations that took place did not occur spontaneously. We had a variety of options for responding to the reactions described in Part 2. We could have continued discussions and tried to achieve consensus before moving forward. We could have responded to the evident resistance by giving up on the approaches being criticized and trying something different. We could have tried to convince our colleagues of the necessity of assessing general education by emphasizing the requirements of the forthcoming accreditation visit.

   We considered all of those possibilities but eliminated each of them. First, we realized that continuing the conversations in their present format would likely never lead to consensus; second, we had considered our approaches and initiatives thoroughly and thoughtfully before embarking on them; and third, we believed that the rationale for assessment is that it improves student learning and the teaching that leads to better student learning. Nothing would be gained and much would be lost by shifting the motivation for assessing student learning to the accreditation visit.

   Instead, we decided to develop models of what we were requesting faculty to do, models that would enable them to see the different modes of assessment in action, relate them to their own needs and situation, and see how others across campus were assessing student learning.

2. Modelling assessment activities provided faculty opportunities to engage with concrete applications rather than abstract ideas.

   We pressed on with three pilots of the student electronic portfolios, not worrying initially or explicitly about their usefulness for campus-wide assessment of the PULs. Instead, we focused on their ability to illustrate the development of student engagement with the PULs during their first year at the university, while building into the technology infrastructure the potential for them to be used for campus-wide assessment. As described in the case, we presented the portfolios from the pilot group and let faculty respond to what they were seeing. The result was the comment quoted about how useful they will be to demonstrate student proficiency in one of the key PULs. Faculty began to see for themselves the potential, but they needed a concrete application to stimulate their thinking in the area of assessment.

   Similarly, the Faculty Associates forged ahead. First, they developed a model matrix for one of the PULs. It showed how the good work of each academic unit could be displayed, while also indicating blanks where work was still needed. Using this model, the Faculty Associates created a full set of matrices, which they presented to the Assessment Committee. The case describes how criticism gave way to understanding and acceptance, culminating in applause for the work of the Faculty Associates. Faculty, and the Faculty Associates, had needed concrete models of what was expected in order to see the possibilities for their own disciplines and their own assessment tasks within the larger context of the campus.

So – what next? At the final meeting of the Assessment Committee for the year 2000, the campus assessment coordinator gave a presentation that distilled the semester's work on the electronic portfolios, the matrices, the school reports, and all the other components of assessment of student learning, showing how each will play a key role as we prepare our self-study for the forthcoming accreditation visit. Most of the questions and comments reflected the distance faculty have come in understanding the role of assessment in improving student learning. But not all.

In response to a directive from the assessment coordinator to 'Please check with your colleagues, in particular review the charge to "set goals for learning in every course and discipline, assess student achievement of these goals, and use assessment findings to improve curriculum and instruction"', one Committee member muttered, 'If it's top down, it won't work.' (This same member had also suggested: 'Well, if we're not there in 2002, we can fake it really well.')

That's the dogma: assessment, particularly assessment that goes beyond evaluation of individual students, is *ipso facto* top down, always mandated by someone else, and never integral to the effectiveness of the teaching/learning process. It is a pervasive belief that is hard to dislodge. Administrators have the responsibility to ensure that assessment of student learning informs curriculum planning and instructional practices; faculty have the responsibility to do it. But it's neither top down nor bottom up; rather it's a working together to achieve more effective student learning.

Our faculty work very hard at assessing the learning of individual students in their classes. They also work hard at planning curricular goals and teaching strategies to achieve those goals. In so doing, they implicitly draw upon their years of experience with and knowledge of what works with students, what skills and knowledge students bring to class, and how they adjust as demographics change and different kinds of students enter their classes. Being used to doing so much of the work of assessment intuitively, they do not see the value of making these implicit curricular and pedagogical insights part of an explicit policy of their own about the role of assessment in teaching – apparently preferring to maintain that it is something that administrators impose on them.

The concrete models that were developed – the matrices and the electronic portfolios – provided an opportunity for faculty to actually see what their colleagues were doing and what students were learning. These were catalysts for starting a potentially productive dialogue about assessing the Principles of Undergraduate Learning. They show the value of taking a second look at the assessment of individual students to see what we can discern about whole classes of students in relation to anticipated standards or principles. But as long as faculty bark at the straw dogma that assessment is imposed from above, and is separate from and in addition to the acts of teaching and learning, the potential will never be fully realized.

CHAPTER 12

TOWARDS A CULTURE OF ASSESSMENT

Case reporter: Kenneth W Borland, Jr

Issues raised

This case deals with the issue of developing a leadership strategy for creating a culture of assessment on a university campus.

Background

The university that is the focus of this case is a US public university that serves about 12,000 students and has nearly 1,000 faculty and academic administrators. Only one-third of its programmes have external professional accrediting agencies that demand assessment of student learning outcomes and only in the past 10 years has the regional accreditation body ('Excellent Schools Association' or ESA) begun to demand the assessment of student outcomes across the entire institution.

PART 1

'Assessment? Is that what we do to students with exams or what they do to us when they fill in the questionnaires on our teaching?' If this was the level of understanding by faculty of what assessment was all about (and for many of them it wouldn't be too far off), we had a *long* way to go to establish a culture of assessment, where the majority understands, values and carries out the assessment of student outcomes in conjunction with the faculty interventions of teaching and curriculum. And it looked as though we would have to tackle this lack of understanding sooner rather than later!

In 1990, our university received a message from ESA. Over the next 15 years, ESA was expecting every member institution first to demonstrate a plan for assessing student outcomes (5 years, by 1995), then show evidence of having conducted the assessments (10 years, by 1999), and ultimately illustrate how the institution was basing decisions in the areas of teaching, curriculum, budget and personnel planning on the assessment of student outcomes (15 years).

Being a 100-year-old 'flagship university' in its state, the university had never before been pressed to prove its effectiveness at meeting its stated purposes or its stated, desired learning and developmental outcomes for its students. It had never considered this a necessity and, in fact, had never formally conducted assessment of learning outcomes across the institution – it had not even encouraged such processes within individual classrooms. The expectation by ESA was thus totally outside of the university's traditional experience and culture, but it had to comply. The saving grace was that, as it had just successfully completed a 10-year ESA review, the university would have time to prepare for meeting the new expectations and (we hoped) to create a new culture of assessment throughout the university. But would there be *enough* time? And how would we do it?

If you were the university's chief academic officer, what would be your first administrative steps toward meeting ESA's expectations?
What would be your long-term strategy?
How would you go about creating a culture of assessment among the faculty?

PART 2

The chief academic officer's first action was to appoint Dr Susan Black to lead the effort to meet ESA's assessment expectations. As Director of Institutional Research, she was capable and highly regarded as a person who knew how to supply decision makers with data. Her new, additional challenge was to get the assessment of student learning outcomes accomplished in a culture that did not understand, appreciate or conduct assessment.

Dr Black's initial strategy was to appoint a task force to develop strategies for implementing outcomes assessment at the university. After considering several alternatives, the task force focused on assessment of learning at the programme level and recommended a programme combining portfolio analysis with standardized testing. It went to the state government for funding to further implement the strategy. However, the funds were not allocated and the strategy was never implemented.

It was then recalled that ESA sought evidence of a programme of university-wide student outcomes assessment. Dr Black converted the task force into the University's Assessment and Outcomes Committee (A&O) and charged it to develop an overall assessment strategy for the university. A&O developed a three-year plan in which:

1. existing assessment activities at the department level would be inventoried;
2. each department would present a plan for what it would soon be assessing;
3. general education faculty would be inventoried to identify desired outcomes for their courses;
4. general education courses would be assessed; and
5. the programme would be expanded to advising and graduate education.

In addition, a 'senior survey' was established to solicit data from graduating students.

Was this the great leap forward? Not exactly – the regional accrediting body applauded the plan because it met their first (five-year) level of expectations, ie it *was* a plan. In most other respects, it achieved very little. After seven years of work by Dr Black, only steps 1 and 2 of the plan were completed. The plan failed to create a culture of assessment on campus. Once departments had presented their assessment plans to achieve step 2, few followed through with action to carry out those plans. Furthermore, the faculty did not 'buy in'. They still were uncertain about what assessment of learning outcomes was and what the personnel implications of such data were; to a large extent they confused assessment of learning with evaluation of teaching. In addition, beyond the traditional grading of assignments, they believed they had no time for assessment of learning outcomes in their heavy teaching–research–service loads.

Moreover, the 'senior survey' had a number of drawbacks. While part of this instrument focused on core general education goals, most of it asked about students' satisfaction with services. There was no university-wide instrument administered in the students' first weeks, so 'pre' and 'post' analyses were not possible. Each College had to find its own ways to increase participation by graduating students, which was usually quite low. Finally, there was no opportunity for a College or any given Department to include survey questions that were specifically related to their desired outcomes.

To top it all off, as the 1995 ESA visit passed, Dr Black left her assessment role to devote her full attention to her work as Director of Institutional Research. So we were left still lacking our university-wide culture of assessment and we still had to prepare for the next hurdle from ESA in five years. What should we do now?

What would you do next if you were in charge?
What do you think actually happened next?

PART 3

In 1996, Professor Barbara Blue succeeded Dr Black as the person responsible for 'all things assessment' at the university. She was energetic and was respected in her field of architecture, but she lacked any knowledge of assessment. However, she quickly demonstrated her capacity to learn about assessment via reading and on-the-job experience. Her main assignment was to get the university ready for the upcoming 1999 ESA 10-year accreditation visit. 'All things assessment' quickly became recognized throughout the university as synonymous with regional accreditation. A&O's work focused on preparing the accreditation document rather than assessment of learning. The administration feared that the university would not have enough of an assessment record to satisfy ESA's next step, simply because there was so little follow-through on and buy-in of the assessment plan established under Dr Black's leadership.

Consequently, the university 'threw money at the problem'. First, a once-only, short-term assessment training event was held. Then the university hurriedly funded numerous assessment projects across the campus. These projects were primarily small in scale, focused on the interests of the faculty members proposing the projects, and not directly linked to the people who made decisions on planning and budgeting. Meanwhile, Dr Black and Professor Blue visited each Department Head. At those meetings, each Head was 'asked' to update the department's assessment plans (Black's step 2) and to report on the outcomes of their implementation. The reason for this 'request' was the impending ESA visit. A deadline was set and most Department Heads complied.

While the presentation of these assessment projects and the reports from Department Heads satisfied ESA, it left Professor Blue in an odd position. She and A&O were overseeing assessment projects that stopped short of linking to decision making and to actions intended to improve learning. She also needed to generate momentum to take assessment to the next and final level of ESA expectations. Working within A&O, Professor Blue attempted to develop a grassroots strategy to establish a long-term plan for assessment that would be owned by the faculty and would lead to broader-based, ongoing assessment of learning outcomes that really resulted in improvements to teaching, learning and the curriculum. She also needed to find something to replace 'the tyranny of the urgent' ESA visit to motivate faculty and to get them to develop and implement an educationally sound programme.

Professor Blue's naturally non-directive approach to leadership, however, led to frustration among A&O members. Most members were assistant deans who defined themselves as not being assessment experts and as being too busy to generate new ideas or to take on additional university leadership work. They attended meetings and responded well to the few concrete ideas placed before them, but they offered little in the way of a grassroots strategy. On one front she did achieve some success. Professor Blue led the senior survey to a new level. The instrument was shifted from a paper and pencil format to an interactive Web-based design. In addition to asking global questions, the survey now permitted each department to include specific questions that would be asked only of that Department's students. As a result, departments got useful feedback; unfortunately, however, the response rate was the lowest in the history of the senior survey.

Out of a sense of frustration with progress on assessment and having additional new university leadership responsibilities on her plate, Professor Blue negotiated the assessment responsibilities out of her job description. So we had now gone through two people and two ESA visits, we still lacked a university-wide culture of assessment, and we had to take our efforts on assessment to a higher level. What now?

What would you do next to try to develop a culture of assessment at the university?
What do you think happened next?

PART 4

The reins were passed to Dr Jerry Green, an assistant professor in a graduate programme focused on the study of Higher Education. In his fourth year at the university, he had been a member of A&O and was an emerging, internationally recognized expert on assessment. He was well aware of A&O's frustrations, but he was not pressured by an impending accreditation visit.

His strategy to create the desired culture was based on the principle of 'management by walking around'. He interviewed Department Heads across the campus and the only item for discussion was his question, 'What can you tell me about assessment from your perspective and how can I be of help?' Those discussions were not welcomed by all Department Heads, but those who did have them expressed a variety of frustrations with a lack of resources, of direction, and of know-how concerning assessment. Yet most Department Heads recognized the value of seeing what was being done and then strategically taking steps to improve so that student learning and development could be enhanced. This was an encouraging sign!

When inevitably asked by the department heads what the university was intending to do now about assessment, Dr Green passed the issue back: 'That is up to your Department to decide.' He encouraged each Department Head to consider five components of an assessment strategy:

1. Determine with your faculty which one or two desired outcomes you wish to assess this year.

2. Check with Department Heads who run similar programmes at other universities where there is a culture of assessment on campus and in their programmes to see how they are conducting assessment.
3. Have your faculty start collecting samples of student work that the students intend to present to demonstrate their progress toward your stated outcomes.
4. Cooperate with me [Dr Green] to get the Department Heads from across campus together to talk and learn about assessment from the perspectives of all of you – what is and is not working at present, what are realistic expectations, how we can reach these expectations.
5. Identify a faculty member in your Department that you would like to appoint as 'Assessment Fellow' to work within your Department and with others on campus to broaden the vision about and improve assessment.

Dr Green then planned a retreat for Department Heads, at which all of the components of the strategy were addressed. At the retreat, Heads of Departments that had attempted assessment of learning outcomes or that had ongoing programmes of assessment that had been mandated by professional accreditation bodies were able to provide valuable insights and guidance to their peers.

Dr Green shifted A&O's role to an advisory one to himself and his assessment direction. One of the first issues before them was how to increase participation in the senior survey. Dr Green urged: 1) that the senior survey be rewritten to focus on the university's and departments' desired outcomes rather than on satisfaction with services; 2) that the senior survey be embedded in every senior capstone course (mandated for every major); and 3) that a uniform, complementary instrument be designed and embedded in every first-year seminar, thus allowing comparison of 'pre' and 'post' data.

Although it is too early to be certain of the effects so far, Dr Green's influence on the university's culture of assessment should eventually be measurable. However, a quantitative impact on assessment processes may be obvious before there is a qualitative effect on the culture of assessment.

What do you think of the outcome?
Do you think that a culture of assessment is now closer to being in place than it had been previously?
What other steps might have been taken?
What are the lessons from this case for creating a culture of assessment at your own university?

CASE REPORTER'S DISCUSSION

Frankly, after almost 11 years, a culture of assessment has still not been fully realized at our university. Yet it is worth reflecting on several aspects of our experience:

- the degree to which the attempt to create a culture of assessment succeeded (or didn't succeed) and possible reasons;
- the alternative strategies and tactics that could have been utilized; and
- the lessons for others from our decade and more of effort.

There is no doubt that, after 10 years of hearing about assessment on our campus, one can find a greater awareness of assessment, and there is some evidence that assessment takes place in some sectors of the university. However, if there is a 'culture of assessment', it may be a *negative* one. Our university completed some good work on assessment and established some frameworks for assessment that served the university well. But being able to do assessment is different from and does not demand a culture of assessment. The university's culture of assessment is on the whole negative and has been shaped largely by reactions to external forces that are considered uninvited, even oppressive. Among faculty and administrators, assessment is viewed as something done because of and for the external forces (eg ESA) rather than out of an intrinsic desire to know about and improve what is done for students (teaching, curriculum) and for learning outcomes. Assessment is a threatening word, still understood by most faculty as 'summative consider-ation of teaching' rather than as 'formative consideration of how to improve student learning'. Our culture of assessment may be changed over a period of time; however, that work will take dedication of time and energy to not only challenge and uproot the existing negative culture of assessment but to simul-taneously introduce and build a positive one. Some of the ways in which this might be achieved are suggested by alternatives that could have been tried at our university and by the lessons we learnt from our experience.

Drs Black, Blue and Green could have more actively exercised initiatives related to faculty development, power and ownership, and unique rather than uniform approaches to assessment. Faculty could have been given more of a sense of *why* assessment had entered their world, *what* it is, *how* to do it, and how it can *benefit* their work in teaching, research and service.

Had they been periodically schooled about the *why* question, their training as scholarly sceptics could have helped them to see the multiple external and internal perspectives that support the work of assessment and that assessment is a cultural value that parallels their own value of seeking to improve knowledge and practice. Had they been taught in their own language (the language of research) *what* assessment is (ie a form of applied research), they might have been more inclined to conduct it. After all, language is a benchmark of culture, and the language of research and the language of assessment are nearly the same. Had they been given guidance on *how* to conduct assessment in the classroom and as teams within their programmes or departments, along with insight on how work on assessment can be used to benefit their teaching–research–service agenda, they would have seen the assessment tools and rewards that match their academic culture.

The issues of power and ownership are fundamental. Had faculty and Department Heads been empowered to design and conduct assessment (ie 'own' the assessment) rather than merely delegated assessment responsibilities (by 'the powers'), I believe a positive culture of assessment would have been more likely to emerge at our university. Finally, a variety of assessment approaches, reporting methods and levels of responsibility could have been considered, rather than the mandated uniform assessment of learning outcomes across disciplines and programmes.

While there are several lessons to be drawn from our experience, I believe there are two major ones. First, top-down assessment efforts are not all that fruitful in terms of creating a positive culture of assessment. A bottom-up approach may not be possible without great expenditure of educational effort. A balanced, top-down and bottom-up, strategy may be ideal. Second, when assessment is perceived as being (or is actually) driven by external forces (be they accreditation, government accountability, or others), the institution's eyes tend to focus higher on the organizational chart than where the students' learning occurs. The temptation is to focus on the level of departments or of programmes within departments, while little emphasis is given to classroom levels of learning or to the individual student's learning. And yet these may be the best places to start creating a culture of assessment.

ASSESSMENT METHODS FOR SPECIAL PURPOSES

CHAPTER 13

But they looked great on paper

Case reporters: Gill Young and Di Marks-Maran

Issues raised

This case study looks at the issue of developing innovative and appropriate assessment methods for a new course that uses problem-based learning.

Background

The programme described in the case was developed at the Faculty of Health and Human Sciences at Thames Valley University, London, United Kingdom. The university is a 'new university', having gained university status in 1992 after being a polytechnic. The Faculty is large, with approximately 300 staff and 6,000 undergraduate and postgraduate, full- and part-time students. The BSc (Honours) Nursing programme had entering classes of 18 students in October 1998, 29 in October 1999 and 33 in October 2000, with students' ages ranging from 19 to 49.

PART 1

'Are we all agreed that we're going to use PBL (problem-based learning) for the new programme? All right, then, how do we propose to assess the students?'

'Er – I take it we won't be using standard written exams?'

'And I think we should be doing more than some of the PBL schools, where assessment is totally in the form of the tutors' ratings of the students.'

'Right on both counts, so let's get down to some serious thinking and planning.'

This was the tenor of our deliberations as we took a journey into new territory and chose to adopt a PBL approach for a new BSc (Honours) Nursing programme leading to both an academic award and professional registration as a nurse. As a Faculty, we already had experience in using PBL in midwifery programmes and some post-registration nursing programmes, but this was to be both our first pre-registration nursing programme using PBL and our first degree-level programme in nursing.

The programme was developed by a group of lecturers and clinical colleagues, with an external 'expert' on PBL curricula in healthcare programmes acting as an adviser. The group developed a modular programme consisting of nine modules, three for each year of the course. The modules were intended to emphasize five themes, ie critical reasoning; assessment and management of care; professional skills; health promotion; and self-development and life-long learning. Furthermore, the overall programme aimed to develop the students of nursing so that they could undertake three key roles:

- **managers of nursing care**, incorporating the individual tasks of assessment, planning, care giving, evaluation, problem solving, decision making, reflecting on practice, providing technical expertise, initiating and/or participating in or managing change;
- **health promoters**, incorporating the tasks of teaching, advising, counselling and communication; and
- **team members**, incorporating the tasks of working with colleagues, leadership and coordination of team activities.

We had thus developed an elaborate programme that was based firmly on the social constructivist ideas underpinning PBL. Our big challenge, then, was to create an assessment strategy that would be coherent with the programme. We realized we would fail if the teaching and learning methods were based on PBL but the assessment methods weren't. In developing the assessment strategy, the planning teams agreed on four principles to guide the choice or construction of assessment techniques:

1. There would be a rich and stimulating mixture of assessment methods across all modules within the programme, to match the richness and stimulation of the PBL programme itself.
2. Assessment would be a vehicle for learning rather than an 'add on' at the end of the learning process.
3. The assessment methods would be congruent with, or reflect, the PBL approach.
4. All assessments would clearly demonstrate achievement by the students of the specified learning outcomes.

So we had what looked like a well-designed teaching programme and a laudable set of principles to guide development of assessment for the programme. But now came the biggest challenge: What actual forms of assessment could we use that would match these high standards?

What assessment methods would you recommend, given the format of the course and the guiding principles for assessment?
What methods do you think were actually adopted?

PART 2

During our discussions, we agreed that, for assessment to be guided by our principles, a variety of methods would be used and the students would have to present evidence of ongoing learning. We looked at the literature from programmes in medicine, nursing and midwifery to identify novel and creative ways of assessing learning in a PBL curriculum. As a result, we developed three types of assessment tool that we believed met the criteria we had specified:

- problem-based case study;
- modified essay; and
- theory–practice portfolio of evidence (for both theoretical and clinical assessment).

We decided that each of these methods would be used in at least one module in each year of the course. The first, the problem-based case study, would require students to identify a critical incident from their own practice and then use the PBL process to present issues arising from the incident, deductions made by the student, evidence-based decisions for care and a reflection on the process and outcome of the incident.

The second type of assessment, the modified essay, would be administered as a formal examination. In it, the students would be given as a trigger the beginning of a case presentation taken from a real patient situation. The students would then be asked a series of questions that reflect the PBL process, questions such as:

- What do you know from this scenario?
- What additional information do you need to find out?
- What suppositions or hypotheses can you make about the patient and the situation?
- What knowledge, information and understanding (evidence) do you need to obtain to test these suppositions/hypotheses?

At intervals, additional information would be given to the students about the patient in the scenario, reflecting changes in the person's condition or test results, notes made by other healthcare professionals who were caring for the person, and so on. This would lead to additional questions being asked of the students. Throughout this dynamic assessment, students would cycle through the PBL process and come up with appropriate nursing decisions that they could justify through evidence.

The third type of assessment would be the theory–practice portfolio, a collection of evidence accumulated over the length of each of the modules in which it was to be used. Students would be given guidelines about the nature of the evidence they should be gathering, based on the specified learning outcomes for the module. The criteria for acceptable evidence would increase in scope and complexity between the first and third years of the course. Material presented by students might include short pieces of evidence-based written work, reflective accounts, analyses of critical incidents from practice, and evidence of acquisition of the key clinical and cognitive skills related to the module. The portfolio would be structured in such a way that students could demonstrate integration of the skills into the theoretical component, application of theory to practice, and generation of theory from practice.

Whew! This assessment programme certainly looked elaborate enough – and, from our perspective, matched the precepts of PBL in demanding self-direction, integration of knowledge and application of information to problems. But how would it work in practice? And what would our students make of it?

What do you think of the assessment instruments that were produced?
What do you think happened when they were used?

PART 3

Although on paper our assessment methods looked as though they should have worked well in our new PBL curriculum, we found that we had to engage in some *problem solving* when we actually used them. First, we had to convert the problem-based case study into a group coursework assignment for students in the first and second years of the programme. This was necessary, as one lecturer put it, 'to get students to do some work in tutorial groups' and was in part a response to poor attendance, poor punctuality and what the lecturers perceived as the students 'not taking responsibility for their learning'. However, there was another important reason for changing the format.

While observing some tutorials in the early part of the programme and interviewing students, we discovered that many students were finding it difficult to adjust to the PBL approach we had designed, and they were not confident that they would 'cover' all the knowledge needed for nursing using PBL. We modified the process somewhat, but we recognized that we were probably expecting too much of the students in the early part of the programme. Because of their difficulties in dealing with the process of PBL, their confidence and ability suffered. We felt that an individual PBL-style case study would be too much to ask for and that a group assignment would be more appropriate. The problem-based case study was retained as an individual assignment in year three at least partly because during that year the students are primarily working in their practice placements. Therefore, group work would prove difficult.

To deal specifically with the problems of teamwork, attendance and student responsibility for learning, a new learning outcome was added for the second module and four new criteria were addressed overtly:

- punctuality and contribution;
- reading, retrieving and evaluating evidence;
- communication skills; and
- supporting peers and the facilitator.

The students assess themselves against these four criteria and discuss their grading with the lecturer during a 10-minute interview. The students' and lecturers' gradings have usually proved to be similar, and the criteria also provide structure for the end-of-module interview. Although sceptics might think it would be impossible for anyone to fail this sort of assessment, there have been some referrals for problems with punctuality and with contribution among the third cohort of students.

The modified essay was never used in the form originally proposed. There were three reasons for this. First, the lecturer who had designed the modified essay left before the programme began. Second, the Faculty introduced a generic examination-marking scheme, which would have proved difficult to use on the modified essay as originally suggested. However, the main stimulus for changing the modified essay was a recognition of the needs of the first group of students in the programme. As already mentioned, some of them struggled to get to grips with both the PBL process and life sciences.

In our new version of the modified essay, we gave the students the scenario – eg a man with chronic lung disease requiring oxygen therapy – on which the final examination questions would be based. We provided this material during the students' 'director of studies' (DOS) tutorials seven to eight weeks before the examination. These tutorials are devoted to developing the students' learning skills. They are timetabled outside of the modules and are provided for all full-time students in the Faculty. During the DOS sessions, students use the PBL process to investigate the given scenario. We also introduced six new topic areas: physiology, psychology, sociology, communication, health promotion, and ethics and professional issues. Lectures that were already timetabled were modified to deal specifically with the examination scenario. Hence it was only the actual examination questions based on the scenario that were not revealed in advance. As one first-year student remarked after the new format was introduced: 'I've never felt so well prepared for an examination.' And how did the students perform? All except one passed the modified essay in its new form, although some required a second attempt. The unsuccessful student from the first cohort was excluded from the programme. These results are consistent with those from our other pre-registration nursing programme.

The theory–practice portfolio has remained largely unchanged from its original design. The practice skills part of the portfolio is essentially the same as that used for our Diploma of Higher Education in Nursing programme and, therefore, already tried and tested. The only difference between programmes is in how the practice skills are structured for educational coherence with each module's theoretical content. However, students in the new programme found the instructions for the portfolio unclear and these were subsequently rewritten in more detail.

Finally, we have introduced an additional assessment to test the students' abilities in drug calculation. This forms part of the students' practice portfolio. A similar assessment has been introduced for all our pre-registration nursing students.

In the spirit of PBL, we have 'learnt' from our 'problems' involving assessment in our new programme. As the instruments and methods are still under development, our conclusions must remain tentative, but it looks as though the assessments we have devised are acceptable to students and staff, are appropriate for the philosophy of PBL, and are achieving their aims of providing feedback to students and teachers and of testing the students' learning.

What do you think of the outcome?
What other steps might have been taken to adapt the assessments to the needs of the students and the programme?
What lessons can you take from this case for developing your own assessment practice?

CASE REPORTERS' DISCUSSION

'Um! Well, it looks like you named it, then you changed it!' That is one way of summarizing our experience of developing an assessment scheme suitable for our new programme taught by PBL. We would prefer to look upon it as an example of adaptability and of responsiveness to observed needs! In fact, writing this case has been an interesting exercise in reflection, as we rarely look back at how our assessment strategies have been adapted once we meet the first cohort of students, or analyse the factors that brought about such changes. Perhaps such an exercise should form part of every new programme's first annual review!

As described in the case, we modified almost all of the assessment procedures that we had designed for the new programme. In theory and on paper, they all looked appropriate and workable, but in practice the responses of our students and our faculty necessitated changes. Therein lie the lessons that we learnt from our experience.

First, PBL is a teaching–learning method that is still foreign to many students, and the additional challenge of novel assessment methods can impose further stress on students. We found that it took some students a full year before they were confident and competent at using the PBL process. We underestimated how long it would take students to adapt to this way of learning, and this led to the need to redesign assessments, especially the modified essay. Nevertheless, we are confident that, given time, the students *will* adapt to PBL and *can* cope with the kinds of assessment that we have devised. When we interviewed our students at the end of their first 18 months in the programme, typical responses to the question 'How do you feel you are progressing on this degree?' were: 'Fabulous', 'Used to system – way of learning' and 'Working better together'. And when they were asked 'Do you feel confident and competent in practice?', they responded: 'I have become confident and competent after a trigger, eg diabetes' and – insightfully – 'Confident yes, competent no, but I know when to seek help'. Lecturers have noted a marked difference not only in how much the students need the lecturers – reducing throughout the programme – but also in what they need lecturers for – with a move from help with the PBL process in year one to help with content in year three.

Second, despite extensive preparation of the lecturers for this new programme with regard to PBL, for most it was a new experience and they, like the students, took much of the first year to gain confidence and the experience needed for competence. A major issue that we debated was how much lecturers should direct students. In retrospect, we feel that many of the students initially needed more direction and structure than we had expected or provided. As our understanding increased about how students learn using PBL, we recognized the need to add more structure and detail to assessment guidelines and processes. As described in the case, these were the main ways that we changed the assessment methods from what we had originally proposed.

Finally, using the DOS sessions (ie learning skills development tutorials) to prepare the students for their examinations by using the assessment scenario and triggers as a focus proved to be a great move. It integrated the DOS sessions with both the module and the assessments and gave the students the support and guidance they needed to cope with what might otherwise have been an anxiety-provoking hurdle at the end of a course that was already stressful enough because of its employment of the unfamiliar teaching–learning modality of PBL.

CHAPTER 14

MAKING THE GRADE

Case reporter: Louise F Deretchin

Issues raised

This case addresses the assessment of individual students in a group process such as problem-based learning.

Background

Baylor College of Medicine is a private medical school in Houston, Texas. Chartered by the State of Texas in 1900, it moved to Houston in 1943 and has become one of the top medical schools in the United States. The College admits approximately 170 new students each year, each of whom has demonstrated high academic performance. A new curriculum was put into effect beginning with the entering class in the fall of 1995. The new curriculum reduced the number of hours allocated to lectures, allowing time for the addition of a problem-based learning course spanning the 18-month pre-clinical curriculum.

PART 1

Well, the crunch had certainly come. Whether I liked it or not, I was going to have to grade the students in my problem-based learning (PBL) group using the new grading scheme. What grades should I give them? And on what basis?

At Baylor College of Medicine (BCM), PBL is a process-driven rather than content-driven course. Students meet in small groups of six to eight with a facilitator, once a week for three hours, to discuss paper-based cases. The students identify learning issues as the case unfolds one page at a time. At the end of the session, each student selects a learning issue or issues to research individually for the next session and then at the beginning of the next session, they discuss these learning issues *vis-à-vis* the case at hand. At the end of each PBL session, the group also conducts a discussion-style evaluation of performance by the group overall and by its individual members. The facilitator's role is to support the students in the process. It is neither to direct the students' thinking nor to be a content source. It is to observe the process and to help the students develop the skills required to solve problems cooperatively, to learn on their own and to learn in collaboration with others in the medical arena.

Still, the students at BCM must be assessed to determine whether they can proceed to the next phase of the curriculum. And therein lay my dilemma. In the PBL course at BCM, there is no prescribed content for which the students are responsible. Therefore, a test of knowledge gained cannot be used in assessing students. The PBL process is very much a group process that is largely out of the control of the individual student. The degree of collaborative interaction is dependent on the group's composition, the facilitator's ability to guide the group into collaborative interaction and the group's willingness to interact.

As a group facilitator, how could I assess students individually on a group process when there is no prescribed content and where the success of the group lies beyond the control of any individual student? Just as for the other facilitators, I had a great deal of autonomy in reaching my decisions. The major criteria for grading had been discussed with all students at the start of the course and on several occasions during it, but there was a good deal of room for subjectivity. Although all facilitators had been given a common form listing typical behaviours, process skills and attitudes to rate, there was scope for great flexibility in how they arrived at their final judgements.

These considerations occupied my thoughts as I tried to decide how to grade Samantha, James and Sam, who were all members of one of my PBL groups. What made this an especially difficult question was the fact that at the time, the course was moving from a 'Pass/Fail' grading system to a finer grained 'Fail/Marginal Pass/Pass/Honours' system. This was happening amidst student cries of rage and accusations that a collaborative process would be turned into a competitive one as students vied for 'Honours'. Course administrators shared the same concern, but the new grading system was mandated – there was no wiggle room.

To top it all off, I was not overly pleased with the progress of this particular group when compared with others I had worked with. This group rarely showed enthusiasm or held lively discussions. I did not sense the camaraderie, mutual stimulation and ease of conversation that come about as a group gels. Although group members seemed pleased with themselves, I would not have given anyone an 'Honours' rating if I were grading the individuals on the basis of the overall group performance. So what should I do about Samantha, James and Sam?

Samantha was intelligent and outgoing. She was thorough in her research and presentation of learning issues. When discussing her findings, she was attentive to the group and whether or not they understood what she was saying. During discussions of cases, she was an eager participant. However, by mid-term, a disturbing pattern had formed. Samantha would present the findings of her researched learning issue apologetically, saying, 'I know I am taking too long. I'm sorry.' She was also apologetic about issues she raised or questions she asked during group discussions. Another feature was that Samantha routinely supported another group member, drawing him into the discussions by saying, 'Tom is so good at this. He has good ideas on this.' While this in itself was admirable behaviour, Samantha was not contributing her own ideas.

During the mid-semester evaluation period when I met with Samantha to discuss her progress, I made two suggestions. If she believed her discussions of learning issues were too long, she might try summarizing them, covering the information to a depth she felt would satisfy the group's needs but leaving room for inquiry. She could keep more in-depth information on hand to be revealed as group members probed further with questions. I encouraged Samantha to continue actively inviting the quieter Tom into the discussion, but to see if she could wean him off relying upon her to bring him into the discussion. Further, I encouraged her to continue to be open about areas where she lacked knowledge but not to be so constantly apologetic.

James was a very confident, bright, MD/PhD student with a wealth of knowledge in the sciences and he was an active participant in the group. His explanations were always clear. More often than not, when questions arose during group discussions, he gave answers with such finality that it ended the budding conversation right there. His knowledge base was excellent, but frequently he made leaps in logic that were error prone. When he discussed a point, it was difficult to tell what was based on fact and what was inference. When someone came up with an unusual (sometimes creative) idea for a learning issue, he frequently made a joke of the suggestion. All in all, he tended to dominate group discussions.

When we got together at mid-semester to discuss skills he needed to address, I made James aware that he needed to work on phrasing his contribution to a discussion in such a way as to encourage others to add to the discussion or to examine further what had been said. I also encouraged him to wait several seconds before answering questions to give other group members an opportunity to participate. And I suggested that in areas where he had more experience and knowledge, he might try using guided inquiry to encourage others towards an understanding. I posed this as an alternative to his being relied upon as a content expert.

Sam was very bright, mature and confident and had excellent communication skills. He had an ability to engage people in discussion, probe ideas and integrate information across disciplines as if there were no lines separating them. He was an excellent listener, quick to pick up on valid ideas and to identify where reasoning appeared to be going astray. All these qualities were in evidence from the beginning of the semester. Sam's participation, however, was patchy. He frequently withdrew from discussion. Early on, he let it be known that he resented the new grading system. According to Sam, a course he had looked forward to attending with pleasure now bore the markings of 'you have to do it for a grade'. He resented being told he had to do something and also the competition this would introduce within the group. He expressed his concerns during a PBL session while the group was evaluating that day's session. Several other members of the group echoed his concerns. I listened to them carefully and then struck an agreement with the group. We agreed that they were not to worry about the grading. They could relax and participate and be assured they would have a Pass for the course. There would be no need to compete for Honours. If the group worked very well together and everyone deserved Honours, everyone would get an Honours rating, despite the recommendation from the administration that the grade distribution roughly resemble a normal curve. My impression was that this recommendation reflected only a vague hope in any event, so I was quite relaxed about abandoning it if such a step would improve the group's performance. This agreement appeared to allay the fears of the group. It broke through a wall and the group could now get on with doing what they needed to do in the course.

As we approached the end of the course, it seemed to me that Samantha and James had responded to the suggestions I had made during the mid-semester evaluation period and Sam had responded to the agreement we had struck about grading. I still was not totally satisfied with the performance of the group as a whole – but how should I go about deciding what grades to give Samantha, James and Sam? What factors should I consider?

What factors would you consider in grading these students?

PART 2

I decided I would factor course objectives, personal values and the student's cognitive and social abilities into my decisions about what grade to give each of them. Rather than viewing these items as separate qualities, however, I considered them to be intertwined, with the students having had multiple opportunities to express them in different contexts. Hence I would give an overall judgement rather than allocating weights to the various criteria. Finally, I decided I would base my ultimate decision quite heavily on what each student had done since the mid-semester evaluation. This is what I had observed for each of them.

Samantha had presented her research on learning issues in a succinct manner without sacrificing the depth of information needed to address the topic well. She invited and was prepared to respond to questions. She also invited quieter members of the group to join in discussion by posing questions directly to them or by inviting them to tell the rest of the group about what they had discussed with her previously. She made her own thoughts and opinions known and contributed to the knowledge of the group. She expressed herself with greater confidence than she had done earlier but retained the ability to come forth with an honest appraisal of her knowledge or lack thereof. She was able to listen to and, when appropriate, question statements by other students in a way that invited further discussion or re-evaluation. She did this in a non-threatening way.

James had worked towards becoming a participant rather than a director and terminator of discussion and did show improvement in that direction. He asked more questions, listened more thoughtfully and inquired more deeply into what others were saying. However, he still had a tendency to declare a discussion over before it was ended and did not differentiate between inference and fact consistently when he presented his own ideas. Unlike Samantha, he never found the appropriate balance between helping others learn and learning from others. He did not consistently recognize the legitimacy and value of others' perspectives.

Sam's participation remained high quality. He was invaluable to the group – an excellent model of how to inquire and contribute ideas, how to think about and use new information. He appeared to continue to struggle with the resentment he held toward the grading system. However, his participation was much improved, though some reserve was still in evidence.

So – based on these considerations and observations, what grades should I give these students?

What grades do you think were awarded?
What grades would you have given?

PART 3

I gave Samantha an 'Honours' rating. I felt that, by term's end, she was displaying the characteristics of a good problem solver, communicator and collaborator.

I awarded James a 'Pass' rather than 'Honours' in the course. I felt that he remained an individual-in-a-group without being able to add the piece that transcends individuality and allows one to use one's individual knowledge and perspective to contribute to others' perspectives in order to build a fuller understanding for all.

I gave Sam 'Honours'. His talent, leadership without dominance and exemplary cognitive and collaborative abilities were superlative. His participation, although not at the full level it could have reached, was outstanding by comparison with others in the group. Overall, I felt that he was operating at an 'Honours' level.

Do you agree with the grades awarded?
What do you think about the reasons for those decisions?
How else might you go about grading students in such classes?

CASE REPORTER'S DISCUSSION

Although still arguable and problematic, the assessment of individual students on a group process may not be as much of a problem as it appears on the surface. In fact, it is an opportunity to observe and assess the individual at a level difficult to achieve in a large group using pencil and paper tests. The method I used in the case is just one possible approach, but I believe that it is a valid and acceptable one.

Typically and traditionally, the individual is assessed at the lowest level of instructional outcomes, ie at the knowledge level – the facts the student has learnt. Bloom identified a hierarchy of learning that begins at the lower levels with knowledge and comprehension (ie facts, concepts and rules are learnt and understood) and continues with higher-level learning: application, analysis, synthesis, and evaluation – where knowledge is used and transformed (Bloom *et al*, 1956). Small group discussion provides facilitators with the opportunity to observe individual students' actual levels of performance – how they seek, integrate, use and communicate information. While some students can comprehend information but have difficulty applying it, others can synthesize information – rearranging or combining old information with new to produce a fuller picture. These students have the requisite knowledge, comprehend its meaning, can apply it in different settings, can analyse the parts that comprise the information and can synthesize information creating a new whole. In PBL, students are asked to act at the highest level of cognitive functioning. They are asked to evaluate not only the validity of new information but also their own approach to gathering, using and communicating information.

Small-group, process-oriented sessions also add the opportunity to observe students' interpersonal skills in a professional environment – how they interact with peers when working on problems in their professional domain. In most cases, it is an absolute pleasure to watch the maturation process as the students let go of the authority–student model and move into the peer–peer model when investigating new ideas. They begin to see learning as a shared activity rather than seeing distinct, non-overlapping roles for teachers and students.

Assessing individuals in a group process-oriented course can be viewed as an overwhelming task. Being clear on what cognitive and interpersonal skills are valued is the first step in simplifying the task. If there is a taxonomy or a theory that meshes well with your understanding of individual cognitive and social development, using it to lend focus to assessing individuals in a group setting helps tremendously. I have found Bloom's taxonomy of levels of learning valuable as a focus. It is a simplified guide to levels of cognitive activity and can serve as a valuable guide for the facilitator about how the student or group needs to be challenged. It also helps to organize cognitive behaviours into categories, thus reducing many individual behaviours into a pattern of behaviours to be observed.

With interpersonal skills, I look for collaborative traits like those I described for the students presented. These include the ability to listen to, use and communicate ideas; respect for and interest in others' ideas; the ability to engage others in the discussion and to ferret out the ideas of reticent partners in problem solving; the ability to critique what is being said in a non-threatening manner; and the ability to receive, evaluate and make good use of feedback.

Once a focus is established, and the attributes and processes sought are understood, then observing behaviours by which to assess individual students in a group process becomes easier. 'Easier' does not mean 'easy'. I have found it to be a challenging process requiring concentration, organization and determination. I have also found the results – the ability to observe students mature in their thinking and interactions – tremendously rewarding.

Reference

Bloom, B S *et al* (1956) *Taxonomy of Educational Objectives: The classification of educational goals. Handbook 1: Cognitive domain*, McKay, New York

CHAPTER 15

READ, THINK AND BE MERRY FOR IN TWO WEEKS YOUR ASSIGNMENT IS DUE

Case reporter: Keith Sullivan

Issues raised

The issue raised by this case study is how to design an assessment that is dynamic, enjoyable and participatory, encourages students' deep learning and can be used in a short, intensive course.

Background

The course that is the focus of this case is a summer semester masters course in education ('Contemporary Education Policy (Comparative)'), at Victoria University of Wellington, New Zealand. Its first half focuses geographically on the Asia Pacific Rim, while the second is a case study of recent education policy developments in Canada. Teaching consists of 11 three-hour sessions conducted late afternoon and early evening twice a week over two summer months. Usually, there is a lecture during the first hour, followed by an hour's interactive tutorial, while the third hour is for individual and group discussions and supervision. The last two sessions of the course are devoted to student presentations. During the second run of the course (December 2000/January 2001), 19 students registered, attended and completed the course – 16 women and 3 men. Students were aged from 21 to 60 and were largely education professionals (teachers, administrators and government employees).

PART 1

In early December 2000, I landed back in New Zealand after having spent five weeks travelling across Canada gathering scholarly materials and information on education policy, and having spoken with teachers, government policy people and university researchers. It had been a lively, full and interesting time. Before I left New Zealand, I had prepared the first section of my course. For section two, I intended to 'fly by the seat of my pants', to create a section that captured the excitement I intended to bring back with me. This would be produced through stimulating lectures and tutorials, and through developing topics and an assessment process to fully engage students' interest.

I was also keen to promote sound learning. I had previously taken part in a research project that found that student self-assessment was a useful strategy for encouraging a deep approach to learning (Sullivan and Hall, 1997). Such learning seemed to be dependent upon stimulating people's interest (so that they focused more clearly) and on providing opportunities to reflect on work done (so that they could improve what they had done or go off on a creative tangent, for instance).

All in all, I was fired with enthusiasm as I prepared to run this summer course – and I hoped the *students* would be as enthusiastic and excited as I was. I believe that course assessment should enhance learning, while encouraging a deep style of learning and being enjoyable. However, when I learnt of the wide range of ages and backgrounds of the students, and of the fact that some would be working or taking another summer course while mine was running, the full challenge of developing an assessment scheme that would meet my goals was brought home to me forcefully. Besides, the whole course was confined to two months – and classes overlapped evening mealtimes. What assessment methods should I choose?

What sorts of assessments would you recommend to meet the various goals and constraints mentioned?
What methods do you think were actually used?

PART 2

Given the nature of the course and participants, I believed that projects or assignments would be preferable to examinations. So I set two assignments, each worth 50 per cent of the final mark for the course. The first, based on the first section of the course (education in the Asia Pacific Rim), was a standard 4,000 to 5,000 word essay on a selected theme from the main topic area. The second assignment was based on the second section of the course (contemporary education policy in Canada) and it was where I introduced elements of more innovative assessment practice.

For this assignment, I combined three tried and true strategies and three new ones to try to trigger deep learning. My feeling was that one strategy on its own wouldn't do this but that the combination might. From strategies I had previously used, I:

- posed an open-ended question with a selection of 10 broad topic areas so as to provide flexibility and the possibility of exploring an area of interest in the Canadian context;
- asked students to work in groups of about three in order to share the limited quantities of resource materials and to discuss and develop their thinking; and
- asked them to give a group 'work-in-progress' seminar as a way of presenting their findings and their thinking to the rest of the class and as a way of getting feedback on their progress. These seminars were to be presented during our last two class meetings and would not be formally assessed. All students were expected to participate in the critique after each presentation.

In addition, as new components, I:

- put boxes of materials for each topic area (articles, books, policy documents I had brought back from Canada or had received in the post) in the Education library for the students to use as the foundation for their assignments;
- provided Internet addresses and materials downloaded from various Canadian sites and encouraged students to carry out a search at these addresses and beyond in order to gather more relevant materials; and
- asked that each student provide a focus question to the class before her or his group presented its seminar, as a means for both directing the student's own thinking and encouraging constructive feedback.

Most of these strategies were intended to foster cooperation among the students in working up their assignments and in providing feedback to each other. I hoped that this would in turn increase their enthusiasm for their work and make preparation of their final product (which was again an individual 4,000 to 5,000 word paper due about two weeks after the group presentations) both easier and more enjoyable.

These plans all looked pretty good to me. But how would they work in practice and what would the students think of them? At least with such a short course, it wouldn't be long before I found out!

What do you think of the assessment methods that were adopted?
What do you think happened when they were used?

PART 3

From my perspective, the assessment methods worked well – but then it was likely that I was biased! I was interested to find out what the students' reactions were, but I didn't want to draw conclusions from my own perceptions of how they reacted. So I devised a voluntary, confidential questionnaire that I asked students to fill out immediately after student presentations had been completed. All 17 students in attendance filled out the form.

In the questionnaire, I asked the students to reflect on the second assignment and to answer the following questions and elaborate on their answers:

1. Was the open-ended nature of the assignment useful or did it make your task difficult?
2. Was the experience of working on the topic in a group interesting, worthwhile and enjoyable or not?
3. Was the process of presentation useful in helping with the assignment?
4. Was it useful to have made up a question about the topic for the rest of the class to consider during the presentation?
5. Was useful feedback obtained from the presentation session?

I also asked them to write any other comments they had.

Reassuringly, between 10 and 14 of the 17 responses were definitely positive for each question. The open-ended nature of the assignment was praised for providing latitude and flexibility. Working in groups was perceived to be valuable for giving access to more information and ideas, making it possible to share limited resources, encouraging self-confidence, extending learning experiences and providing new social contacts. The process of presenting was felt to be useful for helping to focus and organize ideas, to develop a framework for writing the paper, to promote critical appraisal of positions, and to generate new ideas or ways of thinking about issues. Providing a question for the rest of the class to think about during the presentation was deemed valuable in helping the students to focus, providing access to new perspectives, clarifying issues, helping with planning and eliciting useful responses from the class and the teacher. Most students felt that they did get useful feedback from their presentation session, mainly in terms of new information or perspectives, but also positive feedback as a confidence booster. Finally, most of the additional comments were positive reactions to the course as a whole.

Naturally, I felt quite good about these responses, but, as is frequently the case, I think I learnt my major lessons for the future from the negative and mixed responses to the various questions. The main reservations appeared to be about the group process and feedback from the presentations. Four of the students said they did not find the group work useful because it hadn't worked as intended. To quote two of the students: 'We didn't really "work" together.

We met once, debriefed each other on our topics, and decided the order of presentations' and '[I] can see in other groups that it worked well but my particular group [wasn't] terribly communicative. Probably partly my fault.' Another couple would have liked a different process: 'I personally prefer to work by myself then share ideas and ask for feedback and suggestions.'

Several students felt that they had not received useful feedback during the presentations. In some instances, this was directly related to the issue of the question each student was to have submitted before her or his group's presentation. Either the questions weren't answered ('No – my question wasn't answered: probably because people weren't really interested in my topic') or the student hadn't given adequate thought to the question before submission ('[The response to the question was] so-so. My question wasn't terribly thought provoking!' 'I found this hard... in fact I didn't have a question because I felt I would be just having a question for question's sake because I couldn't think of anything worthwhile').

Finally, there was the occasional lament that external circumstances or other commitments had interfered with the student's full involvement in the course. And one student asked: 'What about introducing a group assignment where we could write one assignment as a group and submit it for a group grade?'

These negative or mixed reactions to my course plan gave me plenty of food for thought for the future. Overall, students had liked the group process, but two indicated they preferred to work alone. Should students have the choice to respond to the assignment according to their preferred learning style, ie in a group context or sailing solo? Or were the 'solo' responses expressed because I did not take the time to create a 'proper' co-operative context rather than leaving things loose? How could I improve the establishment of the group process so that it would be effective for all participants? Would it undermine the group process ethos if individuals could opt out and work by themselves? Is it feasible to set a group assignment and have one grade awarded for the group as a whole?

The provision of a focus question helped most presenters to organize their seminars and allowed those listening to provide constructive feedback. Why didn't this work for everyone? What can I do to improve the feedback process?

Clearly, there were variations in the degree of commitment to the course amongst the students. Was this due to some aspect of my preparation or presentation of the course (which I can address next time) or to circumstances beyond my control (eg several students were doing a second intensive summer course at the same time as mine, leading to conflicting demands)?

I believe that my assessment procedure for this course was, on the whole, successful. This was a relief, as I had been concerned about the short, intensive nature of the course and the heterogeneity of the students. Now if I can just build on the strengths and eliminate the weaknesses....

What do you think of the reactions to the assessment procedures?
What are the lessons from the case for the design of assessments in your own situation?

CASE REPORTER'S DISCUSSION

The interval of development of the innovative assessment procedures for this course was almost as intense and hectic as the course itself! And much of the process was designed 'on the fly' and in response to what I observed in the early phase of the course. Normally, a full outline for a course must be prepared before the course begins. In this case, however, I provided a draft course outline to students at the beginning of the course so that I could design the second section (including the assessment) after I had more time to reflect on how best to do this. During December and January, several things were happening. Materials that I had requested from government agencies (by e-mail or through the post) and packages of materials that I had requested or posted while I was in Canada began to arrive. This meant that I was able to select areas where students would have the most up-to-date materials and could ensure that there would be enough of these to provide a foundation for their assignments.

I also started to get a sense of the interests and skills of class members from their introduction of themselves during our first session and through ensuing class and individual interactions. During this early phase, I provided tutorial readings for the course and asked groups of students to volunteer to take responsibility for presenting the tutorials. My thinking here was that teaching others is an effective way for someone to learn a topic and that students are likely to be supportive of each other's efforts when they participate as both presenter and listener.

It soon became apparent from the innovative and enjoyable student tutorial presentations that there were a number of excellent and innovative educators in the class. Furthermore, the way the various groups creatively divided up the responsibilities and presented their tutorials suggested that working cooperatively was proving to be beneficial for both the presenters and the participants. No two tutorials used the same approach. Each was different from the others and engendered lively and relevant discussion (and it appeared that effective learning was taking place). I was able to limit my role in these tutorials to facilitating discussion, subtly re-focusing the tutorial on those occasions when things started to go off track, and calling attention to key issues that might otherwise have been lost.

In view of the wide range of useful materials that had arrived and because of the developing cooperative relationships in the class, I decided to develop strategies for assessment that built on the strengths within the situation. In doing this, I both reflected on what had worked in the past for me and adopted some new strategies, basically by relying on my intuition and pragmatism. One of my strategies, of getting students to present their seminars jointly, relied on cooperative processing and the fact that when you are required to present your ideas to others, you are forced to clarify your thinking.

The questionnaire was intended to find out if my strategies and the overall 'game plan' had worked. From the answers students gave, there was a sense that this had been a worthwhile experience for nearly all of them. Furthermore, the responses suggested that one of my goals – the stimulation of deep learning – had been at least partially realized. As I have already noted, research has indicated that deep learning is linked to providing a stimulus in a way that leads students to focus more clearly on their particular topic, and then giving them the opportunity to reflect on and respond creatively to their chosen topic so that they can claim 'ownership' of it. Responses to the questionnaire suggested that the presentation of seminars and the provision of a focus question for their peers allowed these processes to occur so that deep learning was promoted and students' finished products were enhanced. This conclusion is supported by the high quality of the assignments produced. What is more, I would expect that even those who did not quite grasp the opportunity (eg the student who was uncertain about the reasons for preparing a focus question and seemed to be processing things in a rather convoluted fashion) would probably have done it better the next time, and would then have achieved a deeper learning experience.

As noted, however, there were a few causes for concern. To me the most significant were the reservations about group functioning and cooperation with peers. I realized that, although the groups were working in a cooperative fashion to varying degrees, this was not truly cooperative learning (see Brown and Thomson, 2000). This method is widely used in primary schools, but it is arguably fundamentally at odds with the competitive ethos of grades and marks that underlies university assessment. On the other hand, in the context of some ethnic groups (such as Maori and Pacific Islanders, who together comprised about one-third of my class) and in some contemporary business contexts, group work for a common goal seems to be a very successful strategy (see Sullivan, 1995). This realization has left me with my major question for further development of my course and its assessment: Would it be appropriate to consider full cooperative learning, including joint assignments, in a 21st-century learning context where flexibility and adaptability are key educational themes, thus turning theory into practice?

References

Brown, D and Thomson, C (2000) *Cooperative Learning in New Zealand Schools*, Dunmore Press, Palmerston North, New Zealand

Sullivan, K and Hall, C (1997) 'Introducing students to self-assessment', *Assessment and Evaluation in Higher Education*, **22**, pp 289–306

Sullivan, M (1995) 'Turning the company on its head', *New Zealand Business*, May, pp 22–27

ADDRESSING THE NEEDS OF INDIVIDUAL STUDENTS IN ASSESSMENT

CHAPTER 16

AH!... SO *THAT'S* 'QUALITY'

Case reporter: D Royce Sadler

Issues raised

This case deals with the issue of how students can be made aware of just what constitutes 'quality' in an assignment or other assessment product they prepare.

Background

In Queensland, Australia, a person may qualify as a high school teacher by undertaking a post-degree programme in education. Part of one such programme was the course on assessing student learning that is the focus of this case. It was taught by two people, one of whom was the case reporter, using a combination of large mass lectures (250 students) and small tutorial groups of about 20 students each. Assessment for grading purposes involved two components, a mid-semester written project–assignment of about 2,000 words and a formal short-answer examination at the end of semester.

PART 1

'Do students produce better quality work when they understand the standards that a university teacher works to?' I had often wondered about that, no more seriously than when I was teaching (and assessing) the course on 'assessing student learning' for a group of post-degree students who were training as high school teachers – where they would in turn teach (and assess) their own students. I knew that many students find having their work assessed stressful. I always felt obliged to minimize stress and to demonstrate within the course itself how assessment principles could be translated into good practice. So I put a lot of effort into being as precise as I could about the assignment topic that was part of the assessment for the course – the nature of the task and what I expected. I did not want students to have to puzzle out or guess what the task required. That much at least should be clear. As I saw it, the students' challenge was to develop a quality product.

The specifications that I produced for the assignment ran to about one page. My own challenge was to find the optimum balance between spelling out exactly what I was looking for and leaving enough scope for originality. The last thing I wanted was cloned assignments.

My usual practice was to set out a number of criteria for the assignment so that the students would know in advance how their work would be judged. The criteria in this case were:

- relevance;
- comprehensiveness;
- coherence;
- logical reasoning; and
- presentation.

I put together a brief glossary to explain the meanings of these terms. *Relevance* meant the degree to which the assignment stuck to the topic and addressed the task, without extraneous material. *Comprehensiveness* referred to how well all bases had been covered, with nothing essential left out. *Coherence* meant how well the entire piece hung together. And so on.

The students duly completed their assignments, and I spent a week or so trailing through what they had written. It was relatively easy to judge the high quality submissions, and just as easy the weak ones. The ones in the middle, as usual, gave me the most trouble. There seemed to be two main reasons.

First, there were different patterns of performance. Some pieces of work were sparkling on one or two of the criteria, abysmal on some others, and middling on the rest. To arrive at a mark, I mentally traded off excellence on some dimensions against weaknesses on others. However, the same overall score also arose for assignments that were reasonably good on all the criteria. How fair was it to use the same mark to represent very different sub-patterns of achievement? What purpose was served by collapsing all the information into a single score?

I had another problem with using separate criteria and reaching an 'on-balance' decision. I knew that some university teachers handled this by specifying maximum scores for each of the criteria, then allocating sub-scores for each and adding them up. I found these numerical schemes to work only moderately well. Typically, I felt uncomfortable with the conceptual overlap that emerged between two or more criteria when I had to decide on a sub-score for each of the separate dimensions. Some criteria that seemed to be discrete and distinct in the abstract turned out to blend into one another when I came to actually use them. The boundaries became fuzzy. This seemed to be more of a problem with some assignments than others. I also had a problem with the occasional discrepancy between the story told by the sum of the sub-scores and my global judgement. Which should I trust?

The second reason that I found it more difficult and time consuming to appraise the middle-level assignments was that I felt morally obliged to give students written comments as feedback on their work. In reality, there was always more to be said about mediocre work, because there were so many ways in which it could have been improved. For any assignment that I thought was potentially salvageable, I put a lot of effort into making detailed suggestions. I hoped that students would take these on board for future assignments. I mostly had little that was diagnostic to say to the best performers, because they had got their projects well and truly together. From time to time, it was great to come across one that was better than I could probably have done myself. At the other end of the scale, the weak projects had so many deficiencies that I hardly knew where to start with the feedback. Privately I wondered how these students could have already completed degree studies.

Once the assignments were marked, I distributed them to students during one of the tutorial sessions. Students tended to sit in the same seats each time. On one occasion, a student in the front row said almost immediately that the score I had given her, 13 out of 20, was far too low. I was slightly taken aback by the insistence in her voice, especially when she was unaware at that point of the scores or comments on anyone else's assignment. Most of the other students by this time were looking through their own work and took no notice of this student's comment.

'My assignment is worth a lot more than 13', she said. 'I never receive scores as low as this. Never.'

I asked her what she thought her score should have been.

'I always get 19 or 20 on a 20-point scale. This one deserves the same. My assignment certainly met all of the criteria you specified.'

She was very definite about it – and I was left wondering how to respond.

How would you respond at this point?
What do you think are the issues here?
What do you think happened next?

PART 2

My first reaction was that this seemed to be shaping up as a standard attempt at bargaining for a higher grade. I had experienced this from students occasionally in the past. Some students are accomplished players at haggling. They know how to use body language, have all their ammunition ready, and set out to win. I wondered, 'What is the deal here?' In any case, how could the student know realistically what her assignment was worth? I had had years of experience behind me, setting and marking similar assessment tasks.

On the other hand, maybe I had for some reason simply been too harsh. Perhaps hers was the last one I had marked one night before I dozed off to sleep. My usual self-alert for tiredness was when I became conscious of having read the same paragraph three or four times, still without a clue as to what was in it. Maybe I had passed that point without knowing it.

I offered to grade her work again. I also said that I would have my teaching colleague make an independent judgement without any communication from me as to the reason. My colleague and I had co-taught for many years, so I knew that getting a second opinion would be easy to organize. I said that to make this arrangement fair, I would need two unmarked copies of the assignment so that neither of us would be influenced by my earlier written comments.

She was happy to provide me with these and I agreed to have a fresh look at her work within one week, in time for the next tutorial session. I found that the work was clearly on task. It was also well written, smooth and very readable. It was, however, lacking in penetrating thought and was descriptive rather than analytic. She had engaged with the topic, but not in a way that got to the fundamental issues and principles.

My colleague's independent conclusion was almost exactly the same as my first one. So was my second. I expected that the student might interpret this as defensiveness or stubbornness on my part and collusion with my colleague.

That year, as it turned out, I had given two students a score of 21 because of the superb quality of their work. It was just brilliant. I approached both of them to see if they would let me show their assignments to another student to demonstrate what superb work was really like. I explained that I would do it anonymously and that I would need fresh copies of their assignments, without my comments in the margins. They were a bit surprised but were happy to go along with the arrangement.

When I returned the first student's work, I explained that my and my colleague's separate judgements were basically consistent with my first. She was somewhat stunned and immediately expressed concern. Then I offered to let her see the other two assignments if she wished. I explained that I had obtained the appropriate permissions. She jumped at the opportunity.

'Read the other two assignments and compare them with yours. If you cannot see why theirs are an order of magnitude better than yours, I will be happy to talk with you and explain what makes the difference in terms of quality.'

The next week she returned the two assignments and said simply: 'No contest! I can see what you mean.' This time she made no reference at all to the criteria.

'Do you want to discuss the two assignments with me?'

'No. I'm quite satisfied.' That was the end of the episode as far as she was concerned.

Sitting beside her was another student who had heard the conversations over the previous two weeks. He asked me, 'Please could I read those assignments as well?' Because I already had permission to show them to another student for illustrative purposes, I could see no ethical or practical reason to deny his request, so I agreed.

One week later, he brought them back with the comment, 'I had no idea that this is what you were expecting. I am positive I could do as well as this myself, now that I can see what you were looking for. Can I have another go?'

Instinctively I wanted to agree, but I was conscious of then having to decide what, in the interests of fairness, I should do about the other 248 students in the course. These students had not seen the two exceptional assignments, but I would have no grounds in principle for denying them access. The option of reworking their assignments had not occurred to them, or to me for that matter. I shuddered at the thought of possibly having to scale another mountain of marking once word got around.

In the end, I agreed to give the neighbour of the first student another opportunity to demonstrate what he could do. He accepted that he would not be given a higher grade on the second attempt even if it were warranted. His main aim was to demonstrate what he believed he was capable of. Our arrangement was that he would work independently, without further access to the two sample assignments, and complete the work within two weeks. He had claimed that he could do as well as the sample assignments. As it turned out, he was not far wrong.

How well do you think this situation was handled?
What other options might have been tried?
Why did the exemplary assignments have such a resounding impact?
What are the lessons to be learnt from this case?

CASE REPORTER'S DISCUSSION

Simple though this incident was, and despite the fact that it involved only four people at the time, it had a profound effect on my view of teaching and assessment, and what I built into future strategies. It drove home to me just how many assumptions university teachers make about how our expectations can be communicated.

One of the key assumptions is that specifying the criteria to be used in appraising students' work does two things. It sets students on the right course for shaping the content and structure of their work, and it is sufficient to explain how we intend to score or grade it. This case study shows that, whereas students may well believe that they have 'met' all of the criteria, the fundamental issue has to do with quality.

In a restricted sense, content and structure can be audited. Student and assessor alike may be able to detect whether (as in the example above) all of the content is relevant to the task (with little or nothing that is irrelevant included), whether that content covers all or most of the important issues, whether the treatment hangs together and is not disjointed, whether the reasoning is sound, and whether the presentation is consistent with academic norms.

But in describing the role of criteria in this way, I have expressed the issue in too simplistic a fashion. I used forms of words that broadly imply a two-state situation: *relevant* or *not relevant, coherent* or *not coherent,* and so on. The first student's comment that she had 'met' all of the criteria followed the same line. In practice, most judgements of complex outcomes do not seem to me to be adequately made using discrete criteria. Listing criteria separately invites students to think about *qualities* rather than *quality.* In any event, there is always the possibility that additional criteria should be invoked for judgements about particular cases. Which of us has not felt constrained by a fixed set of criteria that we are confident cannot do justice to a particular assignment? The real issue is that of quality. Quality is determined by how the specified – and the unspecified – criteria are invoked in practice, and how all the various qualities contribute together in concert.

How could I as a university teacher improve my ability to convey to my students a concept of quality? Initially, I had tried to define content and structure in reasonably factual ways, as propositional knowledge. But that was not all there was to 'quality'. The old adage: 'I cannot really describe what quality is, but I know it when I see it' has more than a grain of truth to it.

If quality has to be *recognized* rather than defined, my practices had to be modified accordingly. The only way to recognize something is to 'experience' it in some way. That is what recognition is about, more or less by definition. The way to recognize 'quality' – that is, high quality – is to see it standing out against a background of the ordinary. That is what accounted for the potency of the exceptional assignments in the case study above as vehicles for conveying the concept of quality as it applied to the set task. It was *show and tell.*

The criteria that I specified were relevant to the assignment, of course, but neither of the two students at the centre of this case study expressed the need to debate them. The fundamental problem was one of *standards,* not *criteria.* Any statement as to whether something has or has not 'met' a criterion presupposes some kind of threshold. Telling the students about the criteria identified the key dimensions of interest to me as assessor, but not the thresholds.

Although this case is not about peer assessment as such, it convinced me of the necessity of focusing explicitly on the issue of quality. I now design peer assessment activities to provide students with opportunities to develop not only production skills but also clarity and an improved personal knowledge of what constitutes quality. I expose students routinely to a range of works that display the quality continuum. Those works are authentic and come from other students.

Students tell me that making judgements about the quality of work of the same kind that they are working on themselves is difficult. It is. But by developing these skills, they are better able to monitor and control the quality of what they are producing during the production process. That is, of course, precisely when it matters.

There is another side to this case as well. The documentation for the project assignment in this course was, I still judge, quite thorough. But by itself it did not go far enough. Giving students specifications for tasks, no matter how detailed those specifications, can never go far enough. If I were to formulate a theorem in teaching and learning similar to those in mathematics, this would be it: *Exemplars convey messages that nothing else can.*

As a university teacher, I have long been aware of the clarifying power of concrete examples, illustrations, stories, case studies and metaphors. They help students to understand abstract concepts and to appreciate the relevance of theory.

'Telling' students about assessment requirements often turns out to be fairly abstract to the students. In the past, when normal telling failed to carry the message adequately, I resorted to more elaborate telling. I now try to show them as well. I realize that the same pedagogical devices that I use with respect to the subject matter in the courses I teach make equally good sense with respect to communicating my expectations about the quality of students' work.

CHAPTER 17

LET'S GET THE ASSESSMENT TO DRIVE THE LEARNING

Case reporters: Kay Sambell, Sue Miller and Susan Hodgson

Issues raised

This case focuses on how judicious integration of assessment issues into teaching sessions can alleviate students' anxieties about producing assignments for marking during the early stages of their university careers.

Background

In 1996 the University of Northumbria at Newcastle in the UK first offered a BA Joint Honours degree in the Faculty of Health, Social Work and Education. The degree is made up of varying routes, two of which focus on children and childhood as major themes for enquiry. The students are predominantly women and they enter with extremely varied prior experiences of learning and non-traditional entry qualifications. Most are the first in their families to go to university. Many enter straight from school, with little life experience and low levels of confidence in an academic environment. Class sizes have increased from fewer than 20 to more than 45. Kay Sambell is the narrator of the story.

PART 1

I was ringing Sue, another Course Leader, to arrange a meeting to discuss teaching developments in the introductory theory units for each of our courses on childhood. Normally I felt confident that these units worked well. Today I wasn't so sure. I felt we needed a sea-change, not just here, but to *all* first-year units. However, I wasn't sure that Sue would share my concerns.

She answered the telephone, and we arranged a time to meet. She asked if anything was the matter.

'I'm not sure. I'd like to talk it through with you, Sue. I'm thinking about a few things that other tutors have been saying recently, and I'm wondering what to do about them.'

What had happened to make me feel this way? I had enjoyed being Course Leader, having been lucky enough to work with an experienced and enthusiastic team of lecturers from a range of disciplinary and professional backgrounds, all of whom had always seemed very positive about their contribution to the course. Team meetings were a pleasure. We all really cared about the student experience and felt passionate about our subject: perspectives on childhood. Our students had seemed appreciative, committed to exploring children's worlds, and a joy to work with. They struggled with academic writing and needed a lot of help and direction, but they appeared to try hard and everyone enjoyed the class sessions.

Perhaps it was nostalgia, but times seemed to have changed. Uncharacteristic e-mail exchanges between members of the course team headed 'A Moan' began to lament a lack of student engagement. I decided to convene a meeting to discuss this, and everyone had similar stories to tell. Most of us felt that getting students to talk in class and to participate was sometimes 'like pulling teeth'. The atmosphere of the meeting was one of disappointment, frustration, annoyance, resignation and self-doubt. And it was striking the extent to which much of what was said revolved around assessment. Something one tutor said echoed a general sentiment: 'Nowadays the only time the students seem to care is two weeks before the assignment's due in, when they wander in for a tutorial saying they can't find anything on the topic! It's unbelievable! Everything covered in the sessions has been relevant to their assignment, but they haven't bothered to think about the reading and discussions in them! And at tutorials they appear to expect you to write the thing for them. What they want, of course, is us just to teach to the test. That short-cuts them having to think at all!'

It bothered me that, for some of us, our feelings verged on anger. I realized that I was feeling cross with the students for making our teaching team feel like this, and extremely unsettled that I too felt like blaming the students.

Having got this off our chests in our meeting, we then discussed the issues further. Sue said: 'OK, let's think about what's really going on. What the students don't seem to be getting is the fact that we think every teaching session is geared to help them get ready for the final assignment. We don't run sessions just to fill time, but to develop their understanding and knowledge, so they can eventually tackle the assignment properly. *We* see class sessions as their chance to clarify their understanding of what they have been learning; *they* see them as occasions for us to dish out material that they can give us back in the assignment. We want them to take responsibility for their learning and are trying to offer them a framework to do this. But they don't see the relevance of all this, don't prepare for sessions, and they start thinking about their essays far too late.'

'Yes, that's just it', I'd agreed. 'We see reading, discussion and writing as a single, unified process, starting in week one, but they see an essay as something you start only when you pick up your pen near the deadline. There's a real gap between our viewpoints on what essay-writing is all about. That was *really* obvious in the recent student forum. One of the key questions students voiced at that meeting was, "Why do we have to do class presentations if they're not marked? We'd be much better off putting time into the assignment".'

Now that I thought about it, this also helped explain an incident that occurred while I was running a session on academic writing during the study-skills unit. I had been talking about ways of approaching an essay. One student had persistently and vociferously contrasted university writing with her prior experience of having her written work assessed. She said she felt that her previous tutors had been 'much better' because they 'told us what bits to put in'. I had tried to explain that there was no formula that we could prescribe, and it was a different enterprise here. 'Well, if *you* can't tell me what I should put into my essay, how the hell am *I* supposed to know?', the student had exclaimed.

It had also struck me during our teaching team discussion how Susan, whose children had themselves been through university fairly recently, saw the situation differently. She, too, had talked about student silence, but she had focused on the fact that most were unclear about what to expect, as they're the first in their family to go to university. 'They are extremely lacking in confidence', she said. 'They're really worried about the assignments.'

As I rang Sue I was thinking about what Susan had said. Perhaps we could do more in introductory units to foster students' academic confidence and their approach to learning and assessment. My informal chats with my personal tutees *had* dwelt a lot on telephone calls home, on families' curiosity about what the students were supposed to be learning at university, and on concerns about whether the students would 'be able to do it'. A group I had been chatting to that morning, I recalled, were *really* worried about their capacity to make the grade. They seemed fearful of summative assessment, but they didn't appear to have well-formed study-skills strategies to approach it effectively.

As I reflected on all this, I saw that there were several issues. I was beginning to see how they might be related and even how we might deal with several of them at the same time. Would Sue agree and could we come up with something that would help?

What do you see as the issues?
What would you do next?
What do think actually happened next?

PART 2

When Sue and I met, we discussed our views of the issues we were trying to address. Firstly, we felt that part of the problem was a lack of clarity in the students' minds about what we were actually looking for in quality work at this level, and about what we would regard as evidence. We wanted to help them appreciate effective and appropriate ways of writing about the subject at this level. We also wanted them to see more forcefully how each session helped develop their ideas about the subject, and how they needed to become responsible for their own learning, by becoming much more active both in and outside sessions. We wanted them to see that reading, discussing their responses and writing were all integral and ongoing ways of deepening their understanding of the subject. This process underpinned the production of effective essays, and we hoped they'd realize it couldn't be done at the last minute, nor could the students simply be told what to put in their assignments, as may have been the case in their prior assessment experiences.

Then we mulled over what we should try to do. 'OK, I've got a plan. We all agree they appear to change their behaviour when assessment draws near. Let's put assessment more clearly on the agenda from the outset of each unit. Let's let the assessment drive the learning', I said. 'I don't mean we should teach to the test as the students seem to want us to – simply spoon-feeding them with information to regurgitate back in their assignments. What I mean is: we need to build more explicit discussion of assessment issues into our teaching, to highlight what *we* see as appropriate ways of tackling assignments. What do you think?'

After a long chat, we agreed this might work. We already felt that we made it very clear to the students what they were expected to do for assessment. We routinely published details of assessment criteria and of expected learning outcomes in each unit handbook. But students did not appear to heed them, and they were certainly not coming forward in sessions to open up useful dialogue about them. So we decided to do more ourselves, at least at introductory levels. We saw this as a case of embedding study skills into the course content, forcing the discussion about assessment issues in class. If this was at the expense of covering course content, so be it.

What we decided to do was to introduce various formative assessment exercises and short writing tasks in first-year core units, rather than simply in the study skills unit. Some were designed to try to scaffold students' approaches to writing. For instance, in one unit, each session was designed to allow students to complete activities and writing tasks that they could ultimately enter into a portfolio with a self-evaluative reflective commentary. The sections of the portfolio were structured around stages, culminating in the production of a summative essay. They included, for example, evidence of reading around the subject by preparing annotated bibliographies, peer discussions on observational visits, group presentations to communicate learning and develop a focus, peer feedback, and essay plans.

Other formative assessment exercises involved informal peer assessment and discussion of concrete examples of student writing in class. In one unit, students prepared brief written pieces to bring to sessions, moving from anecdotal, untheorized writing early in the term, through responses to questions designed to allow them to see how to theorize these and to encourage them to practise using key terminology and ideas in their writing. All were circulated for discussion about the degree of application of appropriate academic/scholarly style, allowing students to begin to evaluate different approaches. Eventually, a peer assessment exercise was used, in which students were asked to select, from a paragraph of student writing, an example of a particular grade, by applying the assessment criteria for the summative assignment.

Our hope was that these strategies would be more in tune with many of our students' prior experiences of assessment, which, a tracking exercise revealed, consisted of alternative assessment strategies such as portfolio building and records of achievement rather than 'traditional' discursive essay-writing.

Having now tried them, we do feel that these strategies have helped enhance dialogue and communication within sessions, especially about tutors' expectations. For the portfolio, students clearly try to unpack what the assignment title asks them to do, even quite early on in the unit. They ask useful questions in sessions about how to use theory and how to focus their assignment. Previously, students seemed reluctant to ask, or at least they did not have an appropriate framework within which to discuss assessment issues productively. Now the tutorials during which the written assignment is discussed seem much more informed and useful. Many students come armed with lists of questions to, as they put it, 'find out what we should be doing for each of the sections in the portfolio'.

Students also appreciate the explicit guidance inherent in being 'forced' to write and share their responses to prepared reading for each session. Seeing other people's strategies and discussing other people's perceptions appear to bolster confidence, too. As one student said, 'When you see other people's [writing] you don't feel you're so bad, after all, so it's good to give it a go.' It also allows students to see, in real rather than abstract terms, what the tutor feels typifies effective writing within the subject. During the peer assessment activity, it became apparent that while the tutor laid emphasis upon criteria to do with understanding the *implications* of theories for children's development, many students simply sought to gather and relay information, ignoring some of the most important criteria. This then became the focus for class discussion and students' action-planning.

All in all, then, we feel that students have appreciated and made good use of the opportunities and suggestions we have provided for them to improve their writing skills. At the same time, we believe it has been valuable for them to obtain feedback on their own ideas about appropriate writing within the substantive content of the subject itself.

How well do you think this problem was handled?
What other options might have been tried?
What are the implications of the case for your own programme?

CASE REPORTERS' DISCUSSION

One of the lessons we have learnt from all of this is that our students need time and explicit guidance in making the transition to writing at university. Viewed one way, our strategies paradoxically may appear to foster very dependent behaviour: we are trying to tell students what we are looking for. Viewed another way, we feel the student response indicates that learners are seeing the need, and feeling comfortable, to open up dialogue about academic expectations as a result. Perhaps this is the first stage of becoming independent (Boud, 1995). In short, the first step to *producing* 'good' work is to *identify what counts as* 'good' work in a given context.

The process of essay-writing can be a mystery for many students and may remain so unless they can discuss it and develop their ideas about tutors' expectations. Otherwise, students are in the dark and unable to take control of their own learning. They rely on us to make judgements about their work, like the student who said: 'I've no idea what they're looking for... so I've no idea whether a piece of work I've handed in is going to get a good mark or a bad mark. Sometimes you've worked really hard on it, and it comes back as useless. Sometimes it comes back with a good mark, and I thought it was rubbish. And I've no idea why.'

We would argue that our formative assessment practices do not simply constitute a case of telling students what the assessment criteria are, because, in our experience, that is not enough. We have, after all, been documenting our criteria and learning outcomes in unit handbooks for a number of years, in an attempt to be transparent and explicit about our expectations. Course tutors have been baffled when students still turn in inappropriate work, even after the tutors were blue in the face from explaining the criteria!

What has been driven home to us is that telling students what the criteria are is not the same as genuinely sharing them, because, as in all effective learning, students need to *do* something with the material to deepen their own understanding. In the case of learning about academic literacy, learners need to actively form their own ideas about what matters in assessment, not only by rehearsing writing in less threatening contexts before it 'counts', but also by practising applying and discussing their understandings of appropriate assessment criteria in 'real' situations. As in all learning, feedback on one's ideas in time to adjust one's approach is vital. Perhaps most importantly, we are beginning to find ways of helping 'non-traditional' students form a foundation for self-monitoring the quality of their own work, which more experienced or 'good' learners appear to do 'naturally'.

To help us do this effectively, we need feedback from our students so that we can 'hear' when some are trying to apply inappropriate criteria to their own work, or miss the importance of some criteria we regard as essential. We feel it is important to start from where our learners actually are, rather than from where we'd like them to be, however frustrating or 'time-wasting' this appears from our subject-focused perspective. It is important that our assessment innovations are embedded in the course content. If we feel strongly about encouraging our students to develop their thinking about the subject – and this is especially important when the subject is children's lives – perhaps we can promote these understandings most effectively via assessment. After all, assessment practice is where the 'deep running ought' of any subject lies (Wolf, 1996).

References

Boud, D (1995) *Enhancing Learning through Self Assessment*, Kogan Page, London

Wolf, D P (1996) 'Assessment as an episode of learning', in *Construction versus Choice in Cognitive Measurement*, ed R E Bennett and W C Ward, pp 213–40, Lawrence Erlbaum Associates, Hillsdale, NJ

CHAPTER 18

REFUSING TO LEARN OR LEARNING TO REFUSE?

Case reporter: Tim Riordan

Issues raised

The fundamental issue raised by this case is the tension between a coherent curriculum with defined student learning outcomes and the learning needs of a particular student.

Background

This incident took place in an introductory philosophy course at a US liberal arts college. The title of the course was *Search for Meaning*, and students used the philosophical and literary texts in the course to reflect on their own sense of meaning.

PART 1

She was adamant about not reading the book I had assigned. 'I started reading that novel by Camus, and I can tell I'm not going to like it. I don't need something like this.' She was standing in front of me after class, her voice trembling as other students in the class filed by us, so I suggested we go to my office to discuss her concerns. She agreed, then added, 'But I'm not going to change my mind.'

As we started to walk out of the classroom, I told Jennifer that I had to go to the mailroom first but would meet her in my office in about five minutes. The truth was that I needed some time to think about what to say to her, and I also thought a walk back to my office with her would be a long, quiet, uncomfortable one for both of us. She didn't seem to mind getting away from me at all, and, as I walked down the hall, I started to think about what I was going to do – I was thinking about Jennifer's needs but also my own desire to maintain the teaching–assessment coherence of my course in order to facilitate her learning.

The course was an introductory philosophy course with about 30 students enrolled, and Jennifer was a traditional-aged student in her second year. We were about halfway through the course when Jennifer refused to read the novel, and she had been doing quite well up to that point. As I thought about her performance, I could say that her assignments were generally thoughtful and usually went to the heart of the questions she was addressing. In class she did not often speak in the larger group, but she made frequent and insightful comments in small group discussions. She seemed engaged in the course, and I remembered that she had been particularly impressed with Socrates, in Plato's *Apology*, because he was willing to die for what he believed was the will of the gods. Recalling this made me wonder if Jennifer's reluctance to read the novel was a reaction to the atheism of Meursault, the main character in *The Stranger* by Camus, but I still wondered why she would be so upset.

When I arrived at my office, Jennifer was already there. I started tentatively, 'I'm sorry if the book upset you, Jennifer. Can you tell me what it is that bothers you about it?'

She was not tentative: 'I just think it's stupid. The main character doesn't believe in anything. Why should I read about someone like that?' She had read the back cover of the book, describing the main character, and she had heard other students who had started reading the book talking about it.

My guess about the reason for her objection seemed to be on target, but it was not unusual for students to dislike the character in the novel. They would either find a way to ignore him or criticize him for his attitudes. Jennifer's response was more troubled, so I tried to proceed with caution: 'Sometimes reading about people who see things differently from the way we do can help us rethink our own assumptions and beliefs, or just look at life a little differently. We don't have to like a character to learn from him.'

Her voice was trembling but firm: 'I don't want to learn anything from someone like him, and I'm not going to read any more of that book. Can we just stop talking about this?'

I thought further questioning was only going to make her feel worse, and I was still not quite sure what to propose – especially since we were both well aware that this assignment was part of the assessment for the course. I asked her to give me a day to think about it. She agreed. Now what should I do?

What appear to be the issues here?
How would you respond?
What do you think happened next?

PART 2

After Jennifer left, I took some time to consider all options. I thought about why I had chosen the novel by Camus in the first place, and that led me to reflect on the learning I wanted the students to achieve in the course. The learning outcomes or goals in my syllabus stated that students would be able to:

- identify significant philosophical issues and questions raised in works of philosophy, literature, and film;
- use philosophical principles and perspectives to reflect on the meaning and significance of integrity;
- explore the relationship between philosophical ideas and the context in which they emerge;
- compare and contrast selected philosophical perspectives in terms of their principles and implications for their own lives;
- articulate the line of reasoning/logic/argument used by selected philosophers in arriving at or defending a position;
- consider the impact of the ideas in the course on their own search for meaning and sense of integrity; and
- contribute to the learning of others in the course through questions and comments based on assignments.

These were the abilities I expected the students to develop and demonstrate by the end of the course, so I asked myself whether it was essential for Jennifer to read this particular novel in order to do this kind of learning. I had selected some readings and films for the course to provide examples of figures, actual or fictional, who seemed to live lives of exceptional integrity. They were committed to what they believed and remained steadfast in that commitment despite serious obstacles and challenges. I had purposely chosen figures that represented very different points of view so that students would be required to reflect on multiple perspectives. At first blush, it appeared that Jennifer was not willing to reflect on one of those, thus missing the opportunity to move beyond the familiar and comfortable. Did this mean that she was avoiding the kind of open, thoughtful, and critical thinking so central to the learning outcomes for the course? Furthermore, was her refusal going to compromise the integrity of the assessment requirements for the course?

When I met with Jennifer the next day, I did have a plan in mind, but I asked her first if she had changed her mind or if she had given any thought to an alternative. She said she had but that nothing had occurred to her, so I explained what I was recommending. She would read an alternative text, *A Man for All Seasons* by Robert Bolt, a play that clearly was about the question of integrity, but whose main character, Thomas More, might be more palatable, while still challenging, to Jennifer. She was to complete a worksheet comparing the character of Thomas More to Socrates and explaining her response to each of the characters. After feedback from me on her worksheet responses, she would write a more reflective three to four page piece on how Thomas More served as an example of integrity and how her own view of integrity had been affected by studying the play. In addition, she would view the film version of the play and write what I called a 'film review' with her classmates as her audience and in which she would compare the film with the written version of the play.

The nature and details of the assignments were important because they were basically identical to the assignments the other students were doing, but with a different text as the focus. I was willing to use an alternative text, but I wanted her to do the same kind of analysis as the other students in the class and that reflected the learning outcomes of the course. I felt this would ensure that Jennifer's assessment process would be equivalent to that of the other students. I explained all of this and she had no objections. I still had a concern, though.

One of the learning outcomes of the course was to contribute to the learning of others in the class, and she could not do that if she merely did all of the assignments as an independent project. I expressed my concern about this to her, and she said, 'But wouldn't it be stupid for me to be in class when I haven't read the book everyone is discussing?'

She had a point: what would she do in those sessions? I had emphasized that making significant contributions to discussions required being prepared, and being there would also put her in a position of discussing, or at least listening to, the very things she wanted to avoid by not reading the book. I was stymied for a moment, but then Jennifer made a suggestion: 'I suppose you could let the class read my film review since I'm supposed to assume they're my audience anyway. How about that?'

At first I wondered what would be the use of having the other students read a review based on a book they hadn't read, but then it gave me an idea I hadn't thought of before. 'Okay, but could you do the review a week early so that the students could use it as an example of how they might write their own reviews? They could get a sense of the form with different content.'

'Are you going to tell them it's my review?'

'No, I'll keep it anonymous. In fact, what your classmates learn about any of this will come from you, not me.'

Jennifer took a thoughtful approach to the assignments and completed them successfully. Her review of the film turned out to be quite good and did serve as an example for the other students. She missed two class sessions. The first was the initial discussion of *The Stranger*, and the second was the session in which the students viewed the film version of the novel. She decided to attend the final discussion of the novel, although she didn't say anything during the class session.

At the end of the course I asked each student to identify the experience in the course that she had found most helpful in reflecting on her own search for meaning and sense of integrity and to explain how it was helpful. Jennifer took this quite seriously, and, in her reflection, did explain why she had refused to read the novel. Her father was dying of cancer, and his strong religious faith and that of his family was the primary source of strength for all of them, including Jennifer. She described how much she admired her father's courage. Her comment to me earlier, 'I don't need this', took on a clearer significance for me.

Her reflection did not end there, however. She explained that, after thinking about it over time, she was troubled by her strong reaction to the novel. She wondered why she had resisted so strongly, so angrily. She didn't elaborate on this very much, but it was clear that she was still struggling with her response. She did say that Thomas More, the main character in *A Man for All Seasons*, reminded her of her father and that she had rented the film for her family to watch. She concluded by saying, 'I'm still glad I didn't read *The Stranger*, but maybe someday I will.'

What do you think of the outcome?
What implications does this case have for the integration of teaching, learning and assessment in your own practice?

CASE REPORTER'S DISCUSSION

I can remember that, when I was interviewed for a position at this college, I was asked what I hoped students would learn as a result of studying philosophy. My reply was that I was more interested in how students were able to think than in what they remembered as a result of their study. This attitude certainly affected the kinds of learning outcomes that I have articulated for students, and it shaped the response I had to this particular situation. I pretty quickly moved beyond a concern that the student read the specific text I had chosen to a question about what would move the student toward the kind of thinking her study of that text was intended to foster.

It is certainly the case that some disciplines and courses demand the study of particular ideas, concepts, perspectives, even specific texts in order to get at the heart of the discipline. I am contending, however, that what ultimately matters is not just that students learn *about* a discipline, but that they are able to *engage in the practice* of the discipline. What I cared about in this instance was that the student learn to think philosophically, not just learn about a particular philosopher. In fact, whether she learnt about Albert Camus might not have been important at all.

Too often, it seems, discourse around teaching and assessment begins with what students should study. Focusing on the kinds of thinking we want our students to learn as the primary question changes the direction of the discourse and can make a big difference in what we think our students should study, and perhaps especially what is involved in how they study. In Jennifer's case, I decided that what I had thought she should study would actually get in the way of her developing the learning outcomes in the course, so I changed my mind. As a result, I have been more intentional in my choice of texts and design of learning experiences in relation to the learning outcomes, and more flexible in my use of what I have chosen and designed and in my development and use of assessment processes while trying to meet the learning needs of individual students.

I do not want to give the impression that my approach to this situation was the perfect one, however. Although I think this student did demonstrate the kind of thinking I had expected in the original assignment, I did miss a teachable moment. I have mentioned that the primary conceptual focus of the course was on the meaning of integrity. In her mind her refusal to read the novel was a matter of integrity, although she did not articulate it that way. I did not explicitly encourage her to make the connection between her own struggle and that of the thinkers and figures in the course. That could have been a very productive path to pursue in light of the kind of reflection I wanted the students to develop in the course. I could have assisted her to consider how she was not refusing to learn, but learning to refuse.

In retrospect, I also think it might have been wise to ask her if she needed to speak with a college counsellor. I could sense that her struggle was a profoundly personal one; that is why I did not push her to say too much about why she refused to read the novel. I tried to walk a fine line between respecting her privacy and beliefs and seeking information in order to make appropriate decisions about her learning. There are times, however, when a student needs help beyond what a teacher can or should offer. As it turned out, it seems that Jennifer managed to handle her struggle, but it would have been wise to suggest the option of counselling. It is clear to me that we cannot ignore the affective and personal dimension of experience in helping our students learn; this situation shows how profoundly those things can shape student learning. For me, the question continues to be how to recognize and address those aspects of learning in ways that are most respectful, constructive, and appropriate; and this is related to the second issue at the heart of this case for me.

It is not a startling revelation to say that students come to their learning with different backgrounds, attitudes, aptitudes and feelings; but using this insight to inform teaching and assessment can be a complicated matter. As in Jennifer's case, it means that materials or experiences that might be very instructive for some students are not helpful for others. It is also true that what works with one group of students does not work so well with another.

This insight has meant that over the years I have become more flexible about the course plan I have. Based on what I am learning from student performance, I am willing to modify the learning experiences and assessment methods I have planned to meet the learning needs of the students in the class. I am also much more likely to provide options for students; that is, instead of assigning one novel, story or essay to the entire class, I will let them choose among two or three.

I had at least one advantage with Jennifer: she told me that she was having difficulty. I did not know exactly what the problem was, but I did know that I had to consider the issue. Students are not always so explicit about their learning difficulties or about what helps them learn, so this experience pushed me to take more initiative in trying to understand who my students are in relation to the learning I want them to achieve. In fact, this involves what I take to be a rather critical assessment principle: ongoing assessment of student performance is essential in order to get a sense of how our students are progressing in relation to learning outcomes.

This implies that assessment is more than an opportunity for evaluation of students. It also provides an opportunity to help them learn through feedback and for the teacher to reflect on the learning processes that will be helpful for them. The experience with Jennifer and others has made me more vigilant in my attention to student performance of all kinds. The comments they make or questions they raise in class and their written assignments can provide means for assessment; they can sometimes reveal as much about how students are progressing with respect to learning goals as more formal assessment opportunities.

As I reflected on my approach to Jennifer's situation, it became clear that I needed to ask myself what would take her the next developmental step toward the learning outcomes of the course. I am not suggesting here that learning is a straight linear process, but the question of what will assist a student to move forward in learning seems to be critical. In this instance it seemed to me that insisting she read the assigned novel would have led her to drop the course. Would that have been in the interest of her learning?

One could argue that she might learn the consequences of not following the rules or of standing up for what one believes, and perhaps those would be valuable lessons. In this case, I decided to focus on the learning outcomes for the course and create an opportunity to address them with a different text from the one I had planned. It also struck me afterwards that it was good to let her know that what I was really interested in was her learning, not whether she would follow my rules. Students are probably more likely to develop as learners when they think their teachers are not just gatekeepers but people who are very interested in helping all of them learn, no matter what it takes.

This leads me to what is often the first question I am asked about this situation. What about the other students? Is this fair to them? My position on this is pretty clear, although I know some would debate it. As I have emphasized, the issue for me was what would help the student develop in relation to the learning outcomes of the course, and this would be the case for any student. The standards of performance are the same for all of the students; how they learn and demonstrate them will vary. In this context, being flexible about the path to learning seems more important to me than making sure that everyone does exactly the same thing. In fact, that is something I try to assist the students to understand as well.

Finally, because I have shared this with my colleagues as a stimulus for reflection on our teaching, my experience with Jennifer provided an opportunity to improve the learning and assessment agenda for many students – not just one. At Alverno College, faculty regularly collaborate and use the experiences they have encountered during their teaching and assessment as a way of assisting one another in curriculum and course design, including the design of assessments. Thus the incident with Jennifer became as much a learning occasion for the wider faculty and other students as it was for myself and Jennifer.

HANDS-ON ASSESSMENT: EVERYDAY PROBLEMS IN ASSESSMENT PRACTICE

CHAPTER 19

WHY DID THEY GET MORE THAN I DID?

Case reporter: Chris Davies

Issues raised

The issue raised by this case is how to deal with the variability in marks that results from team teaching and assessing a subject.

Background

First-year engineering students at Monash University, Melbourne, Australia, study a common course before specializing in a chosen discipline for the remaining three years of their studies. Laboratory classes are considered to be a vital part of the course, and consequently up to 300 first-year students must be accommodated each week for each subject. The subject I teach – Materials Engineering – is taught on two campuses by two academic staff assisted by a team of 16 to 20 tutors drawn from postgraduate and final-year undergraduate ranks.

PART 1

Students taking Materials Engineering are assigned to lab groups consisting of about 14 students, and each group is assigned a single tutor for the whole semester. As part of their assessment, they must submit reports on seven experiments and these are marked by the group's tutor. The full-time teaching staff had prepared marking schemes and we tried to ensure that tutors understood the schemes. We also had regular weekly meetings to brief tutors on the week's lab. All in all, we were reasonably confident that this part of the assessment procedure would run smoothly. We were very concerned, therefore, when we started getting feedback from the class that things were not going according to plan. There were mutterings that students in some groups were being 'short-changed', that reports of equivalent quality were receiving very different marks, and that some tutors were perceived to be more lenient than others in their marking. What was going on? Was it a real problem? What should we do about it?

How would you address the issue?
What strategies could be employed to deal with variability in the marking of the reports?
What do you think happened next?

PART 2

Even a brief look at the distribution of marks convinced us that there was indeed more variability than we would have expected. Something had to be done! The first thing we did was to ask the tutors if they could explain the uneven spread of marks in the class. They suggested that the key factor was the interpretation of the marking schemes drawn up by the full-time teaching staff. Alan said: 'We understand what to do when marks are allocated to specific tasks: it's clear what you mean when one mark is allocated for correctly using an equation, or two marks for correctly plotting a graph. But what do you mean when, for example, you allocate five marks to "the discussion"? What's a sensible discussion? What differentiates a good discussion from a bad one?' He concluded, 'We can't tell what's in your head.'

Now we had something to go on. Next we had to find a way to minimize differences in the ways in which markers perceived the marking scheme. We already had the meetings to discuss the procedure for the week's lab, so why not expand these to team meetings during which the group would agree on the performance criteria for the various degrees of achievement for that week's report?

Over the mid-semester break, I organized a seminar for tutors. I explained my plan and the reasons for it. I gave each tutor a copy of a six-page book extract on establishing marking criteria. Tutors were asked to read the outline for the week's experiment before the meeting and write down a list of their own criteria. At each meeting we would then agree on a common list of criteria that would be used to guide the marking and could be handed out to the class to demonstrate that the marking was being done fairly. Simple, no?

No. The first meeting was a nightmare. We certainly generated a lot of discussion, but the tutors' opinions fell into one of three groups. The first group did not see the need to develop marking criteria at all and were represented by the view of one tutor: 'I can only decide how to distribute marks when I see the reports.' The second group was 'process-driven' and had based their criteria on the elements of the report. This was very much in line with previous marking schemes and included marks allocated for 'introduction', 'correct results', and 'discussion' without any guidance on how a marker should decide whether to award a high or a low mark. This group's scheme also included what I call 'make-work' marks, such as two marks for correctly labelling axes on a graph. The third group *did* attempt to develop criteria based on achievement. They suggested, for example, that full marks would be received for correctly identifying and quantitatively ranking the various sources of errors in the experiment – correct identification of the error sources but incorrect ranking of them would receive a lower mark. At last! Something we could work with. Based mainly on contributions from this third group, we developed a set of performance criteria for the first lab, and by the end of the meeting I thought we were well on our way to reducing the variability.

When the marks came back from the tutors, it was clear to me that we still had some work to do. Most marks were between 65 and 75 per cent – around the 70 per cent dividing line between a 'credit' and a 'distinction' (B plus to A minus) – but the students in three groups received an average mark in the 'high distinction' range (80 per cent or greater). I had expected that it would take some time for tutors to get used to the new scheme, but at the same time I knew that the groups with higher marks would be the ones that would provoke the most complaints from fellow students.

At the next meeting, I pointed out the inconsistencies, reminding tutors that students ought to be able to expect that their work would receive more or less the same mark regardless of who was doing the marking. At that meeting, I had the impression that we did a better job of establishing the performance criteria. However, when the next set of marks was returned, the variation was still there, with the same tutors marking consistently higher. Just as I feared, during the two or three days after the reports were handed back to the class, I was confronted by several students asking why they had received lower marks than their classmates in another group for what they thought was the same work. What to do?

What do you think accounts for the ongoing variability in the marking of the lab reports?
What would you do in the face of this persistent problem?
What do you think was done next?

PART 3

I found this state of affairs very disheartening and at the next meeting asked the tutors for their explanation of the situation. 'I followed the criteria, and that's what I came up with', was a typical response. Kate – one of the tutors I thought was happy with the new scheme – said, 'I find it's easiest to mark when marks are given for a calculation or a question, but I agree it's probably not as good as using the criteria we've established.' Other tutors echoed this. 'It's difficult to interpret the criteria', or 'Thinking about the criteria takes more time', was typical of the mood of the meeting. Most of the tutors were familiar with the previous scheme – either as tutors in previous years or as students – so I asked them which they would prefer to use. Overwhelmingly, they chose the old scheme, in which marks were allocated for tasks. However, when I asked for comment on what they perceived to be the negative points of their preferred scheme, most of the tutors agreed with Jane, who said, 'It's easier for us to explain what areas are important to write up and it makes marking a lot faster, but it also makes it easier for students to pick up marks without doing all the work.' Then Kate said something that really took me by surprise. She explained that she thought tutors were doing different things both during and between the lab sessions: 'We cross-check our marks in the fourth-year room, and some of us get our groups to stay for the whole two hours to ask questions, but some tutors let their groups go after they've finished the experiment, and [when this happens] they have no idea how to answer the questions or write up the lab report.'

While changing the assessment policy, I'd uncovered more than I'd bargained for, and clearly, interpretation of the marking scheme was by no means the only factor affecting students' marks: how the tutors behaved was also having an influence.

In the end, three issues emerged as sources of difference among the tutors:

1. Time was a concern for most of the tutors as all have significant responsibilities other than their tutoring job – mainly their research or their own studies. Several (but not all) tutors made themselves available for consultation by students between lab sessions, and this paid dividends for their groups in leading to better marks. While this would seem to be the professionally responsible thing to do, tutors are casual staff, paid only for time spent in the classroom, for marking, and for preparing for and attending the weekly meetings. Crucially, tutors were not expected to be available between classes, and those who were doing this were in effect donating their time.
2. Some tutors, but not all, had formed themselves into sub-groups in which they 'compared notes'. This contributed to an agreed interpretation of the criteria and to similarity among marks awarded, which is the outcome we were seeking.
3. All of the tutors were familiar with the 'old' marking scheme, and most were unfamiliar with the new. The new performance criteria were more holistic than specific, and this was identified as the main problem when it came to interpreting the criteria. It was difficulties with this interpretation and the higher marks given to some groups that hadn't received 'extra' attention that sparked off the whole exercise.

I'd like to be able to say that everything was resolved after we recognized these issues, but it wasn't. Some things could be fixed immediately: the criteria for subsequent reports were made more specific, and tutors were directed to encourage their group to ask questions after the experimental work was completed. (This worked better for some groups than for others.) Time constraints were more difficult to escape, and while we'd have liked to run sessions at which all tutors could mark as a group, this proved impossible to arrange. As a compromise, tutors were asked to submit copies of what they considered the best and worst reports from their group so that their marking could be moderated, but this was only partially successful, again because of time limitations. However, extracts from these reports served as examples not only for tutors but also for students in helping them understand the descriptions of criteria the next time the same lab was run. Budget constraints restricted the employment of tutors between lab class sessions, but a 'senior tutor' position was created and part of the brief for this person is to answer students' enquiries related to the labs. Finally, to train each year's crop of new tutors, we expanded the introductory seminar to incorporate workshop activities: practice at criterion development and subsequent marking of example reports against these, followed by discussion of the marks awarded.

By far the most significant improvement has been that when students now question their marks, we can point to the criteria for that particular report. 'Why did they get more than I did?' becomes 'Where did I fail to meet the criteria?'

How well do you feel the situation was handled?
What are the implications of team teaching for assessing large groups?
What are the lessons from this case for your own practice?

CASE REPORTER'S DISCUSSION

Variability in marking is probably one of the most contentious issues that academics have to deal with, and it was because of negative feedback in this regard that we attempted to implement a system that would define in some detail the level of achievement required for a particular mark. An important feature of this is that it must be transparent, as students being able to read what they must do to obtain a high mark is a powerful motivator.

The initial concerns expressed by the tutors are common to both novice and seasoned markers. In my experience, many marking schemes are vague, with considerable latitude given to the markers' 'feel' for the work in front of them. While this might be adequate for a single marker assessing a few reports, even over a period as short as a few hours – say, the time it takes to mark 20 lab reports – the things that attract marks when the marker finishes the task may be subtly (or even strikingly) different from those that received marks when he or she sat down.

It is not unreasonable to question why we hadn't noticed the differences between tutors independently of students bringing the matter to our attention. In fact we had, but we didn't have a basis for an alternative until I went on a teaching course and learnt about performance criteria. Our previous 'method' had been to monitor marks and suggest to tutors that they seemed to be marking a bit high or a bit low.

Indeed, prior to introducing the current scheme, I had received two suggestions from colleagues about how to eliminate variability in marking, both of which I rejected. The first proposed normalizing the marks based on an average of the average marks from tutors, but this strikes me as being unfair, penalizing the truly good students if they happen to be in a 'good' group. Our aim was not to standardize marks in any way; rather we wanted a rational basis for allocating marks. Alternatively, I was advised to allocate reports to tutors independent of the group they tutored, but this strategy appears to be designed to hide the problem rather than to rectify it.

While students will always compare marks, individuals are rightly concerned with one mark only – their own. When they make comparisons with their peers they are seeking to confirm that they have been treated fairly. These comparisons are fraught with difficulties. For instance, the degree of coaching given by a tutor will influence the mark. Ensuring that students understand the lab before leaving the classroom and the tutor's availability for consultation can both act to raise a student's mark. The central issue must be that all students are treated fairly. However, there's no such person as a 'standard tutor', and in our case, rather than forbid tutors to talk to students between classes (I am loath to discourage enthusiasm!), we have opened up alternative avenues for consultation between sessions for those students whose tutors are unavailable. Similarly, performance criteria show students what they must do to achieve a certain mark.

One thing that hasn't changed is that we still get students querying the mark they were awarded, but the questions now are usually for reasons other than the perceived leniency of a tutor. Again, this points to the need for a fair, transparent and rational means to allocate marks, and comparison with a set of performance criteria is likely to be less subjective than comparison with a colleague. None the less, intrinsic differences between groups are, I think, unavoidable. I would expect that if a group's reports were to be re-marked by a different tutor, the average mark for that group would not change, but I would *not* expect a comparison among groups to yield the same average mark for each group. There are two reasons for this: our groups are relatively small – 14 members or fewer – and the membership is self-selecting – to a large degree students choose who their lab mates are. In fact, when we compared lab marks with test marks, there was a weak but positive correlation between average lab mark and average test mark (for a machine-marked multiple choice test) for a given group.

In reflecting on this case, I have realized that it is necessary to distinguish between what might be called 'legitimate' and 'illegitimate' factors accounting for variability in marks awarded. The 'illegitimate' ones – differences arising from interpretation of a marking scheme – are the ones we sought to eliminate and are the main focus of this case. However, variation will also arise as a consequence of the behaviour of the tutors and/or students during the conduct of a lab and this effect is 'overlaid' on the interpretation of the marking scheme. Tutors who make themselves available between class sessions and thereby improve their students' knowledge and/or understanding are 'legitimately' contributing to the variation of marks – although it would be best to ensure that all students had access to such assistance. Consequently, variation in marks cannot be completely eliminated. All we can do is temper the 'legitimate' causes – for example, as we did when we introduced the senior tutor role – while trying to eliminate as much as possible the 'illegitimate' ones.

CHAPTER 20

BETWEEN A ROCK AND A HARD PLACE

Case reporter: Phil Race

Issues raised

This case addresses issues about the role of the external examiner, and about managing disagreements between internal assessors.

Background

The incident described in the case occurred in a professional development programme at a large university in the UK. The situation arose before and during the meeting of the examinations board at the end of my first year as external examiner for the programme, which was in its first year of operation in its current form.

PART 1

I had been an external examiner for professional development programmes for many years and saw no problem in taking on the role for a large, new programme. I had been talking to the course team informally for some time as an unofficial adviser; I helped with the design of the programme and, more particularly, its assessment framework.

Part of the assessment for the professional development programme consisted of two written assignments, partly case-study in nature, which were double-marked (separately, unseen) by members of a team of assessors from several different disciplines. The assessment criteria for the assignments were related closely to the published learning outcomes of the programme. For each assignment, there were eight such outcomes to be evidenced, and for each an assessment judgement was made separately by each of the two assessors, with a pass/fail decision being entered on a pro forma, and further feedback provided separately by each assessor to the candidate. For an overall pass in either assignment, each of the assessment decisions had to be a pass, showing that all of the learning outcomes had been satisfactorily achieved. The third (and main) element of assessment was a portfolio providing evidence of the professional practice of the candidate, the portfolio being assessed in a manner similar to the assignments.

The work of the candidates was in general of a high standard, somewhat higher than in most similar programmes at the same level in other universities that I know. Where the two assessors agreed that the overall verdict on an item of assessment was a pass (the most frequent occurrence on this large programme), there were no problems. Where both assessors agreed that an assignment had failed, it was normally sent to me as external examiner for a further opinion. Usually (but not always), I was able to confirm the decisions of the internal assessors for both clear pass and clear fail assignments. Sometimes, however, the two assessors did not agree in their assessments. The procedure then was for each of them to be alerted by the course leader to the assessment judgements and feedback comments that they had written separately, and for them to be asked to try to agree. In addition, my view was sought as an additional factor to be considered by the team. Because of my perceived availability as an adjudicator for cases of disagreement between internal assessors, some of them tended to dig in their heels in such cases. They would stick to their respective arguments about why they thought that an assignment warranted a pass or fail decision and then look to me to provide a rationale for my own decision.

It began to dawn on me that, despite having quite clear assessment criteria matching the published learning outcomes, the cases of disagreement often arose because the internal assessors were bringing their own 'baggage' into play when making their judgements. For example, some assessors were quite preoccupied with looking for correct grammar, spelling and referencing in the assignments and in the portfolio, while other assessors were looking primarily for evidence of good professional practice and were less concerned about the details of language and presentation.

At the exam board, the assessments of candidates' portfolios of evidence were considered along with those of the assignments. Here, and now face to face with me, some assessors who had failed assignments on the grounds of grammar, spelling and presentation became quite defensive about their decisions to do so. When I suggested that some of the failed assignments would have been passed at other universities I know, they argued that they were defending the standards of their own university and that it did not matter if those standards were higher than elsewhere. Indeed, they regarded it as a virtue that the standards *were* set higher.

One instance summed up the problem quite sharply. A candidate whose portfolio was the focus of this kind of internal assessment disagreement had included a copy of an e-mail communication to a trainee, but the e-mail message had several spelling errors in it and was somewhat clumsy grammatically. One assessor thought that such a level of use of English could not possibly be accepted on a programme at this level, while the other asserted that the e-mail was perfectly clear as far as the message to be communicated was concerned – it was just an example of a quick, informal communication.

At the meeting of the board, several of the borderline cases still rested on such issues. The internal assessors present once again stated their conflicting views and looked to me to make a ruling on each of the cases affected. Although the cases of disagreement represented only a small fraction of the candidates considered by the exam board, the causes of the disagreements took up most of the time and energy of the board. And I was to be the 'meat in the sandwich'. They were looking to me to decide the issue and whatever I did could cause anger or resentment. I was between a rock and a hard place. What should I do?

What would you do next?
What should be done about the balance between professional practice and grammar, spelling and referencing in assignments and portfolios?
What approach should the course team take over the procedures for handling disagreements between internal assessors?

PART 2

Whatever my personal beliefs about the relative importance of the content and stylistic components of the assessments, I believed first and foremost that the decisions should rest on the faculty's own guidelines and processes. Accordingly, my advice at the exam board included the following observations and suggestions:

- At the time of this incident, there were no explicit learning outcomes concerning the quality of spelling, grammar and referencing in candidates' evidence. Therefore, where candidates had met the stated learning outcomes relating to professional practice, they should not be penalized for other things. They could still be given *feedback* about those other things, but the assessment judgement should not be affected. If it were considered desirable, for the next run of the course, one or more learning outcomes could be added addressing the grammatical and referencing side of candidates' evidence, but they should not apply during the current run.

- Where there were disagreements between internal assessors, the programme needed a better method of resolving these, rather than resorting to the external examiner as an adjudicator (apart from exceptional cases). Internal assessors should be more firmly encouraged to reach agreement, and in cases where this was still not forthcoming, a third internal assessor should act as adjudicator. I suggested that the programme would not be able to move towards improved inter-tutor reliability unless the problem regarding disagreement was addressed openly within the entire assessment team.
- As the professional development programme involved candidates in producing evidence of their own skills in designing and implementing assessment, it was necessary for the programme itself to address the issue of consistency in its own assessment processes.
- As some of the problems could be attributed to variable quality of the mentoring that was provided to candidates in the programme, the programme needed to be made less dependent on the level of support that would be available from mentors. Alternatively, all mentors needed to be required to be more closely involved, for example by looking at candidates' evidence *before* it was submitted for assessment and checking it against the assessment criteria and learning outcomes.
- Rather than have pass/fail decisions on each learning outcome and each assessment criterion, it would be better to have 'strongly met', 'adequately met', 'nearly met' and 'not yet met' decisions, and for the overall assessment decision of pass/fail *not* to require that each and every sub-decision be favourable. In this way, assessors could choose to concentrate their overall decision on the more important learning outcomes relating to professional practice.
- It would be useful to introduce an element of self-assessment. For example, if candidates themselves completed a checklist showing the extent to which *they* considered they had met the learning outcomes, and supplied this along with their work, it would be less likely that candidates would fall short of addressing the outcomes explicitly.

As the incident described occurred only recently, it is too early to say whether these suggestions will help to solve the problems to which they relate. However, the idea of one or more 'third assessors' being brought into play was received well, as was the suggestion of allowing candidates to assess themselves against each criterion, as a further indication of their own reflection upon their work. There was some discussion about whether certain learning outcomes were 'core' and others 'marginal', and whether only the 'core' ones should be taken into account when making the pass/fail decision.

My formal report to the university concerned was, of course, much more general. I long ago found that the time to make real suggestions to a course team is during informal communications along the assessment highway, rather than as a glorious cacophony at the terminus! Even the mildest of critical comments, when delivered in a formal report, can cause course teams to have boiling oil poured upon them from great heights in some UK universities!

How well do you think this situation was handled?
What other suggestions might have been given to the course team to deal with the problems?
What are the implications of the case for your own practices in assessment?

CASE REPORTER'S DISCUSSION

Many of the lessons to be learnt from the experience recounted in this case are suggested by the observations and recommendations that I made to the examinations board. For the most part, they are related to two important general issues: the criteria for assessment decisions and the reliability of marking. Just as in the incident described, I believe that situations involving disagreement between assessors frequently arise because, in the first place, 'learning outcomes' have not been written in language that is helpful to students as 'goalposts' for their learning. This lack of clarity or specificity then makes it difficult to establish strong links between learning outcomes and assessment criteria. If the assessment criteria are only loosely related to outcomes and if, in addition, the criteria are inadequately defined or inadequately understood by students and/or assessors, problems with inter-rater reliability can almost be guaranteed.

Experience elsewhere has confirmed that assessing assignments and portfolios using double marking (blind) shows few disagreements about good work or about poor work, and that, as in the case described, the problems occur with borderline instances where some of the learning outcomes have been met more successfully than others. It has also been found that where there are several learning outcomes to be taken into account to reach a single assessment decision, different assessors are likely to have conflicting views about the relative importance of the different outcomes.

Simplifying the learning outcomes and the assessment criteria might appear to be one solution, but this can have the effect of leading towards reduction, or to a situation where only the unimportant things are taken into account by the assessment. It is always harder to make assessment decisions about the extent of achievement of complex and high-level learning outcomes, but in a professional practice programme, this is more important than merely attending to that which is easy to assess. It is dangerously easy for academics to (consciously or subconsciously) assess the language of a written piece of evidence rather than its substance.

One other difficulty associated with decisions on higher-order criteria in assignments like those described in the case may be related to the outstanding quality of the best assignments. Perhaps assessors need to be reminded that the purpose of programmes like the one in the case is to accredit *competent* practitioners, rather than outstanding ones. In the case, all of the candidates came across to me, through their words, as at least competent, even where their written evidence in meeting particular criteria was more patchy.

Still, there *are* ways to help assessors in their judgements even on high-level criteria and learning outcomes. One that I suggested to the course team involved in the case was a visual grid, which could be made available to assessors to help them make pass/fail decisions. It could have the various criteria listed in one column, alongside relevant descriptors in adjacent 'should' and 'should not' columns. For example, for the criterion 'bringing in relevant current literature', the related 'should' column might list: '10 or more sources, most within last five years, at least some sources mainstream educational writers, appropriate quotations made linking to context in assignment'; the 'should not' column might list: 'use only two or three sources, use "old" sources (eg where authors have proceeded to later, more-developed writing), use only idiosyncratic sources that candidates happen to have noticed, quote literature in a vacuum, unrelated to context of assignment'. Such a device could well help assessors reach more consistent conclusions, although it would have to be well thought out and carefully constructed for some of the more abstract qualities or criteria.

A further point at which disagreements between assessors might be confronted is the final judgement itself. In the incident described, I felt that the 'pass/fail' decision at the end of the pro forma could have contributed to some of the problems by being too 'hard'. Disagreements might be softened if the overall final decision could be, for example, 'clear pass/borderline pass/borderline fail/clear fail'. Assessors could be allowed to 'fail' assignments on one or even two criteria, but award an overall 'borderline pass' by allowing compensation for significant strengths in the 'passed' criteria.

In the final analysis, perhaps one of the key solutions resides in effective faculty development. At least some of the problems with inter-rater reliability could be reduced if *all* the assessors could be persuaded to spend half a day at an assessment workshop, assessing in parallel carefully planned case-study pieces of work (planned to contain most of the problems that they are likely to meet in practice). But it seems well nigh impossible to sell the idea to some experienced academics that they have anything to learn about how to assess. And even this approach would not test the deep waters of *intra-assessor* reliability: the consistency with which the same assessor would pass or fail the same piece of work on different days.

CHAPTER 21

STANDARDS + DISTANCE = TROUBLE?

Case reporters: Keith Miller and Liz McDowell

Issues raised

This case study focuses on some of the difficulties that arise during implementation of outcomes-based assessment in placement settings that are also at a distance from the university teachers.

Background

UK Government policy now requires student teachers on a PGCE (Postgraduate Certificate in Education) course to spend much more time in schools than previously. Nevertheless, the university running the course retains ultimate responsibility, albeit in partnership with teachers in schools, for supporting and monitoring students' progress towards gaining Qualified Teacher Status (QTS). Keith Miller narrates the case.

PART 1

That's it – I've had enough! I was almost on the point of giving up – or at least at the stage of seeking help and support. Not only were we going to have to deal with a new outcomes-based assessment scheme for our trainee teachers, but we were going to have to do it at a distance. Then the University chose to 'rationalize' so that I was the sole member of the secondary science education team remaining! How was I going to cope?

For many years, the University of Northumbria had organized high quality teacher training courses and because University faculty retained control over the programme, they were able to keep the training tight and focused. However, things were changing due to new national requirements for teacher training. Student teachers would be spending two-thirds of their time in school placements away from the University and all trainee teachers would have to meet a set of newly introduced Standards before they could be awarded Qualified Teacher Status.

This new national set of 'Standards for Initial Teacher Training' is a series of outcomes-based statements identifying the knowledge and skills required by students before being awarded QTS. I had concerns about using such an approach, although I felt that transparency of learning outcomes could benefit student teachers by helping them focus on clear outcomes and know what was required in terms of assessment criteria. My worry was that it could be used badly, the danger being that students might adopt a mechanistic 'ticking-off' of outcome statements rather than developing as well-rounded and informed professionals having a sound knowledge and values base.

I could readily envisage student teachers unthinkingly stuffing lesson plans and photocopies of articles into plastic wallets to be submitted as a portfolio at the end of the course. I had seen pupils in schools do this on some vocational courses – without active engagement in the process or any critical or reflective dimension. I have always felt passionately about the importance of teaching and was concerned that if new teachers failed to develop insight through reflection on important principles and processes, they might be reduced to having sterile and technical approaches, without a love for learning and without the underpinning sound foundation that is necessary. I was not convinced that the Standards would lead to the ends I sought.

To further complicate matters, the time that I would be able to spend in direct contact with students and their mentors, either in the schools or at the University, was from now on going to be very limited. I was concerned that without my ongoing support, enthusiasm and desire to promote what I felt were positive attributes, these beginning teachers would not enter the profession with the necessary underpinning values and knowledge that would allow them to become a credit to the profession.

As I saw it, then, my main problem was: How could I get the trainee teachers to understand and then use appropriately the new outcomes-based assessment programme? And how could I do it almost entirely at a distance, since I could spend little time with individual students at the schools where they were placed?

What steps would you take to help the placement students understand outcomes-based assessment?
What do you think was actually done?

PART 2

My major concern was to ensure that the assessment of the Standards in schools was rigorous and consistent and that the students were keeping sufficient and appropriate evidence so that their standards claims could be verified. Of course, this meant that students had to understand the outcomes-based assessment system first! I was not surprised to find that many of the new student teachers had no experience of an outcomes-based approach. They expressed concerns about a range of issues, such as: 'How much evidence is needed to show that we have passed the Standard?' 'Do we have to do each Standard several times or is once enough?' 'If we have done this Standard before the course, can we claim it?' 'Who is going to pay for all the photocopying of our notes and lesson plans?' 'This isn't what I came into teaching to do.' 'If you don't want us to photocopy all our notes and lesson plans and then put them in a portfolio, what *do* you want?' 'Where is our relationship with pupils recorded?' 'Isn't it our enthusiasm, organization and ability to motivate pupils that is important, yet this isn't easily measured?' 'This is a bureaucratic farce!'

I decided that I really had to quell some anxieties before they got out of hand. I concluded that adequate induction would be particularly important, especially since I could capitalize on the initial period when the students were based at the University. During the induction programme, I introduced the students to the 'Standards' in as non-threatening a manner as possible. Then over a period of weeks at the start of the course, I revisited the Standards, discussed the process of collecting evidence and explained the role of tutorials in the course. Eventually, the initial panic subsided to a state of mild concern.

The student teachers decided that they would focus on good practice first, try to teach well in school, reflect on their learning and then claim what Standards they could from these experiences. Identified gaps would then have to be addressed through later University- or school-based sessions. At first, many of them feared that the assessment of so many Standards would result in its being a 'bureaucratic nightmare' to compile their portfolio evidence. I worked hard to avoid this! I provided documentation to give a framework, on paper and electronically, that would help them manage and reference the volume of evidence they needed to link their achievements to the Standards. There was, however, an ongoing concern about when 'enough was enough'. As one student said, 'This is driving me crazy. I want to make sure that I pass, but I'm not sure how much evidence you need to have in order to check that I have passed each Standard. Do I have to just do it once or several times?'

After several sessions and partnership meetings, the students, their school mentors and University tutors seemed to achieve a good common understanding of the Standards statements, but the issue of the volume of evidence remained a problem. In the end, I told the students that they had to trust me to be working on their side to identify achievement and that I would also take oral evidence from them. It helped several of the student teachers when I explained to them my gate-keeping assessor's role in that I had to ensure that it was only competent teachers who would be allowed to enter the teaching profession.

The steps I had taken appeared to soothe the students' anxieties and they seemed to have developed a reasonable grasp of the Standards and of outcomes-based assessment. But now came my next challenge, and it was a big one. How would I be able to monitor their achievements and provide support when they were scattered far and wide in their school placements?

How would you go about monitoring the teacher trainees' progress while they were working in schools well away from the University?
What measures do you think were actually employed?

PART 3

It was at this point that I thought more seriously about one of my other dreams for the course. I was keen to promote the effective use of Information and Communications Technology (ICT) in the classroom, believing that it has considerable potential, when used well, to improve the learning experiences of pupils. Why not start with their budding teachers?! I contacted Liz McDowell, who was coordinating a University-wide project using ICT to support teaching and learning, and asked how the new technology could be used to help me maintain contact with students and schools. Eventually, I decided to make use of some relatively 'simple' technologies, mainly e-mail, electronic discussion lists and the Web. I even ran a session on making simple Web pages – with some interesting spin-offs. One student was initially very nervous about using the technology but after producing a small Web-based package in the first session was able to report: 'I have really gained street cred with my sons. I went back home this evening and showed them how to do Web pages using Word and saving as html… they were really impressed!'

A bonus of using ICT this way was that, as part of the Standards, student teachers have to demonstrate personal competence in the use of ICT and use ICT effectively in the classroom to support teaching and learning. Mentors in the schools recognized that they would have particular difficulty in supporting these outcomes because many did not have the ICT skills themselves and were making little use of ICT in the classroom. By making ICT part of the course process, I would directly assist students to achieve the required outcomes and help mentors to develop their skills, too. ICT became an important part of the induction programme and ongoing training for students.

I found the direct e-mail contact with students invaluable and students also appreciated being able to contact me and other students directly. Regular exchange of e-mails kept me up to date with what was happening, enabling me to monitor individual students' progress and providing indication at an early stage of any emerging problems or issues. I devised a tracking summary sheet that students sent to me as an e-mail attachment, ensuring that I was kept informed of their progress towards meeting the Standards. It was particularly satisfying when a Government-appointed Inspector asked: 'How do you monitor the training and progress while student teachers are on placement?' In spite of my own personal beliefs that this mechanistic approach was detracting from some aspects of development and creativity, it did give me some satisfaction when I was immediately able to show him the up-to-date assessment and progress details for each student!

The students reported finding the electronic discussion groups particularly useful. As one said: 'I really loved the e-groups. They were brilliant. Although not everyone communicated, it was really helpful to know how the others in the group were feeling. I had such a laugh at some of the comments and it helped me to realize that I wasn't the only one feeling stressed out.'

On the whole, then, I felt reasonably satisfied with the outcome. The students appeared to feel comfortable with the assessment system, they could be monitored and supported from a distance, and they were getting experience of using ICT. And I was finding (with relief) that a one-person 'team' at the University *could* cope. What more could I ask for?

What do you think of the outcome?
What other forms of ICT might have been employed? How?
What are the lessons from the case for your own assessment practice?

CASE REPORTERS' DISCUSSION

In the United Kingdom, many qualifications, especially vocational ones, now use outcomes-based assessment approaches, allowing students to collect material from a range of sources to provide evidence of achievement. Many of the student teachers on the PGCE course described in the case, however, had not come from vocational settings and the introduction to the Standards proved quite a culture shock. The students were used to assessment methods that relied heavily on end-of-semester examinations or submitted coursework. The notion of claiming Standards through evidence gathered in university and school contexts was foreign to many and at first provoked anxiety and concern among them. As described in the case, Keith, the tutor, worked particularly hard to clarify things for the students before they moved from the University to their attachments in schools.

Despite his efforts to 'sell' the Standards to the students, one of Keith's initial concerns had been that the Standards might be used as a definition of all the important elements and that higher-level professional skills might be neglected. He felt there was a potential problem in that student teachers could leave their final placement as a 'clone' of their last mentor and that they could have mechanistically ticked off the Standards without gaining a holistic understanding of the professional role of the teacher. A review tutorial both in school and at the University became an important part of the formative assessment process, allowing discussion of achievements, and humanization and focusing of the training to meet the needs of individual student teachers and of the Standards. The final section of the Standards focuses on wider professional qualities and it is in this section that some of these higher-order teaching skills were addressed and promoted.

One of the PGCE students helped to alleviate some of Keith's concerns about how the Standards might be used when he wrote: 'Our Standards assessment was in no way mechanistic. It involved a holistic reflection on the teaching practice, at specific points, and utilized statements of Standards to help both student and mentor to focus on the achievements at hand. The tick-box system helped me to identify the "gaps" in my practice so that I could improve and develop as a "whole" teacher and then plan activities that could be assessed and accredited to those standards.' While this may not have been the case with all the students, it did suggest that it was good practice that drove the system rather than students planning disconnected activities in order to address discrete elements in the Standards. This was quite a relief to Keith as he sought to ensure that the sum of a professional teacher's skills would be greater than the discrete parts as measured in a series of competence statements.

In addition to meeting the teaching Standards, student teachers also have to achieve the ICT-related Standards. The routine use of ICT to communicate helped to reinforce skills that could then be claimed for the Standards. There were, however, problems with this at both the University and school ends. First of all, there were teething problems with the University system that was used. Students were given names to log in with and passwords on registration, but not all of the students had these and several students couldn't get them to work. Unless everyone was able to access the e-mails and public folders, we wouldn't be able to use the system and we would have to revert to slower 'snail mail' or abandon this approach. The prospect of this disappointed Keith, because he thought that ICT had considerable potential to improve and maintain relationships with students and show good practice that would be crucial for the next generation of teachers. Fortunately, this 'worst-case scenario' didn't eventuate.

While ICT access may have been difficult for some students while on campus, it was particularly problematic when they were not at the University. As one student said: 'How can I read my e-mails when the only computer in the school is in the office and it is only administrative staff who are allowed to use it?' Some students agreed, however, that it was more their own level of organization and establishment of routines that was a problem. One said: 'There is a computer in the staff room that is there for us to use and I confess that I just haven't got myself organized to log in regularly. Sorry, I will do this from now on.' The initial two days per week placements allowed students to try out the systems in schools and then feed back any problems to Keith at the University for remediation. One exercise that was undertaken was for the students to send Keith an electronic version of their CV and timetable so that he could check on who could do this successfully. He could then prompt or check with those who hadn't done this and find out the barriers. Was it lack of confidence or competence in ICT – calling for extra classes – or was it other issues surrounding motivation, organization or access?

Despite the promising start to the work with these students on outcomes-based assessment, there are several questions yet to be answered fully. Have we proven that there are benefits in introducing the Standards at the start of the PGCE teacher training course? Could the volume of the assessment in terms of portfolios, logbooks and tracking documentation be reduced? Is the transparency of the required learning outcomes combined with extensive discussion of best practice a useful model or have we merely trained student teachers to 'jump through hoops'? Does this model help student teachers' motivation and enthusiasm for further professional development or is the mechanistic process of checking off the Standards perceived as an end in itself?

The answers to at least some of these questions should begin to emerge as we discuss the strengths and weaknesses of the processes with the student teachers and as we gain experience with the new ICT and assessment systems based on the Standards. Our hope is that new teachers will become well-rounded professionals who are able to develop good relationships with students and who can apply a range of teaching and assessment methods that promote enthusiasm for learning and the development of high-level skills. Only time will tell whether this approach to initial teacher training will achieve these goals.

CHAPTER 22

ORGANIZED CHAOS

Case reporter: Melissa de Zwart

Issues raised

This case raises the issues of how to deal with a missing item of assessment and how flexible a teacher should be in accommodating students making the transition from secondary school to university. It also highlights the value of effective office management.

Background

The incident described occurred during the 1990s in the Law Faculty at Monash University, Melbourne, Australia. 'Legal Process' is a course for first-year law students and is regarded by most students as a basic introductory course. The class size at the time was about 350 students per year, divided into eight streams of 40–45 students each for this course.

PART 1

The incident was almost as much of a mess as my office. I even worried that my messy office might have caused it! It was a year during which I was teaching two streams of Legal Process for the first time. One stream was my own; the other I had abruptly 'inherited' partway into the course from a teacher who had to fill a gap in a later year elective. The assessment that year was a court report, a research assignment and the end-of-year exam. The problem arose with the research assignment.

With so many students and so much activity, I had allowed my office to fall into a state of chaos. When the research assignments arrived, I had suddenly acquired 55 papers to grade on a topic I knew nothing about, in addition to the 50 plus on the topic that I had set for my own stream. Scattered around the office, I had lists of students who had done oral reports, lists of students who were yet to complete this piece of assessment and an administrative nightmare in the form of over 100 folders, binders and scrappy pieces of paper, on top of my own piles of unfinished lecture notes and research.

Some weeks had passed in second semester and the students were becoming anxious about getting their research assignments back so that they could see how they were placed for the end-of-year exam. When I finished grading and prepared to hand back the assignments, I noticed that one was missing. I could find no record of having received or marked the research assignment of one student, Meg, who I knew had attended class and was still enrolled in the subject. I immediately felt guilty, believing that my messy office was to blame. I turned the room upside down in a frantic attempt to find the missing paper. The search proved fruitless.

I was still keen to hand back the marked papers that day. Rather than wasting further time looking, I obtained Meg's phone number and rang her at home. 'Did you hand in your assignment?', I asked; 'I'm sorry, but I'm afraid I can't find it.' At this stage I was feeling very guilty, thinking that I might have misplaced the assignment. I was at least comforted by the fact that the assignment instructions had specifically required the student to keep a copy of the submitted assignment, both in hard copy and on disk. She confirmed that she had submitted an assignment. I asked her to print out a duplicate of the assignment and mail or bring it in and she readily agreed.

Some time later, she telephoned back. She said: 'I apologize about this, but I can't find the disk with the final version of my assignment. All I have is a disk with some rough notes and research. What should I do?' By this stage I was starting to suspect that the assignment had not in fact been completed. I said: 'That's all right; I'll be happy to look at whatever evidence you've got that you've completed the assignment.' At the same time, I asked: 'When and where did you submit the assignment?' The majority of the class had handed in their assignments in class, with a few students bringing them directly to my office. She explained: 'That day I was sick, so I gave the assignment to one of my friends to hand in. But she said she couldn't find you, so she put it in your pigeonhole. I'm quite sure the assignment was turned in all right.'

Well, as far as I could tell, it wasn't in my office and I couldn't find any evidence of it anywhere. What should I do now?

What would you say or do next?
What do you think actually happened?

PART 2

I asked Meg to come to see me in my office. I am a firm believer in the need to establish a personal basis for communication with my students. In these days of growing class sizes and fewer tutorials, this is becoming increasingly difficult. I have frequently found that students who require extensions of time for submission of assessments or who have not performed well in assessment have very serious personal problems that they are reluctant to discuss. In fact, sometimes mid-year or mid-semester assessment acts as an alarm bell for the teacher and the student, indicating that help or intervention or good old-fashioned hard work might be necessary.

Later that day there was a knock on my door and Meg appeared. I was relieved, as I had been concerned that she might not show up at all. 'How are you?', I asked. I avoided asking why she had not been to class in the last few weeks, as I did not want to put any additional pressure on her. 'I'm okay now, but I've been sick. I don't think I've been studying hard enough and I've also been devoting a lot of my time and energy to a musical project that some of us students have going.' I talked with her further about this and explained that it was quite normal to have problems in using time effectively. She seemed to relax when talking about the musical project and I believe this fostered an atmosphere of mutual respect.

After chatting with her for a while, I asked what records she had of the research she had performed. Finally, she confessed that she had not submitted the assignment, that she had started to do it but had never completed it. All she had was some notes. I think I was more upset about the situation than Meg was. I felt very sorry that she thought she had needed to lie, but I was immensely relieved that she trusted me enough to tell me the truth. (Of course, I was also very relieved that I had not lost the assignment in the jungle that was my office!)

I then had to consider what to do next. I said: 'I'll give you an extension of time to do the assignment, but I won't be able to give you anything more than a pass for it, given the time that has elapsed. And I want you to sign a declaration that you won't look at any of the assignments that I've already marked and returned.' She agreed and I made a time for a follow-up meeting to assess her progress. She started attending classes again.

Ultimately, she decided not to complete the assignment but to devote her effort to obtaining a high mark in the end-of-year exam. I was concerned about the risk involved in doing this but had others in the class who had failed the assignment and thus were in almost as bad a position.

Meg did well in the exam and obtained a pass grade in the subject despite having lost the entire 20 per cent of the final mark allocated to the assignment. She went on to complete her degree. She later came to see me and said that at the time of the assignment, she had been sick and disillusioned. She had contemplated dropping out of law altogether but my encouragement had spurred her on to do well in the exam. This had given her the confidence to continue her studies.

How well do you think the situation was handled?
What other actions might have been taken?
What would you have done in the same situation?

CASE REPORTER'S DISCUSSION

Apart from the obvious example about personal organization, this incident taught me some valuable lessons. The first is the importance of devoting the time and effort needed to get to know students on an individual basis. Our Faculty works to keep class size in first-year subjects to a minimum for this reason. However, some students are more demanding than others and some simply fall through the cracks. For this reason I consider it very useful to have assessment spread out over the year, rather than focused entirely on the year-end, by which time some students may be well and truly beyond saving.

Our difficulty is accentuated by the nature and timing of the Legal Process course. Most students regard this first-year subject as a basic introductory course that is easy to pass. Most of the students have come into the class straight from secondary school, full of enthusiasm. They have got into law, the course of their choice, they are high achievers and they 'know' that they are going to get a good mark in this subject because students from the later years in the curriculum have told them it is easy. Many students therefore do not take assessment in the subject seriously. In addition, they are often distracted by their first year of freedom as university students. They do not have teachers keeping close track of their progress and they are free of the pressure of having to get high scores at the end of the year the way they did to gain entry to law school. All of these factors combine to provide some unique problems in assessment.

In first-year subjects I try, therefore, to set two pieces of assessment in the first semester, and I have found that it is at this time that I can identify the student who may need to be referred to student counselling, the writing skills teacher or the librarian. Assessment at this stage of the course is at least as much formative as it is summative. Some tasks that are purely formative and carry no weight can also be set, but students quickly learn what they 'have to' do and what is 'optional'. One alternative is to describe some tasks as hurdle requirements that must be completed but carry no marks.

Since the incident described, I have implemented a much more rigorous system for submission of assignments, including double-checking of submissions received every day and follow-up letters two days after the due date. I recently received an e-mail message from a student asking for his results in a subject in which he had attended all of the classes but had submitted no assessment. I was able to say with confidence that neither piece of assessment had been received and that he had not responded to a follow-up letter. And I was not even tempted to dig around in my office looking for his assessment.

CONCLUSION

In the introduction to this book, we pointed to the unprecedented level of change that is currently sweeping through higher education worldwide, especially in terms of massive increases in student numbers, widening in the backgrounds and diversity of students, and the development of more flexible approaches to teaching and learning, including the use of information technology. The introduction highlighted the crucial importance of assessment in linking the learning objectives of a course, through its teaching and learning activities, to the eventual learning outcomes demanded of students. Each case in the book has grappled with some aspect of these 'big picture' issues in particular curricular or institutional contexts. By way of conclusion, we offer a short reflection upon some of the major issues that appear to us to have emerged from the cases.

GENERAL IMPLICATIONS OF CHANGE

Many cases examined the implications of change in terms of, for example, the introduction of information technology (*Taking the Byte Out of Computer-based Testing, Gain without Pain?*) or movement to an institution-wide system of assessment (*Barking at Straw Dogma, Wading Through Glue, Towards a Culture of Assessment*). General implications of change from these and other cases (*Assessing Reflection or Supporting Learning?, But They Looked Great on Paper*) include:

- acknowledgement of the systems theory perspective that changing one small aspect of assessment can have unforeseen and sometimes major consequences elsewhere;

- the seeming impossibility of 'getting it right first time' and the associated need for a number of iterations;
- the need for a comprehensive approach towards major change (eg teaching and assessment of generic attributes are best developed for a whole curriculum rather than a specific course);
- the fact that the availability of resources, especially hardware and software, always seems to lag behind what is needed to complete each phase of change.

IMPACT OF CHANGE ON FACULTY

Associated with the general implications of change is its impact upon, firstly, the change agents themselves. Cases such as *IT to the Rescue*, *The Reflection Jigsaw* and *Portfolios from Cyberia* make compelling reading because of the 'angst' and frustration they have caused the innovators. Often, rather than being acknowledged for their leadership, change agents find themselves signing up to confront problem after problem.

One of their major problems is the resistance of other faculty members to change. Of course, change in itself is not necessarily always good. But neither is it necessarily always bad, and the reader may want to reflect on the validity of the reasons for faculty resistance to change presented in the cases. A common problem is that of moving from a situation where some staff have developed good skills (eg in the design of multiple-choice questions) to one where everyone has such skills (so that, for example, all questions are strong across a whole course or programme, eg in *What to Do about John?*, *Gain without Pain?*). The move towards quality assurance for a whole course, programme or institution is a difficult one for many institutions to make, as it can be perceived as detracting from academic autonomy and as a matter of 'top-down' management control (*Barking at Straw Dogma*, *Towards a Culture of Assessment*). Other cases (*Wading Through Glue* and *The Reflection Jigsaw*) report happier collegial outcomes from such a process.

INSTITUTIONAL POLICY

The impact of institutional policy is seen in various ways. For example, the need to meet the demands of external accreditation or quality audit has necessitated the development of assessment policy across whole programmes (*Wading Through Glue*, *Barking at Straw Dogma*, *Towards a Culture of Assessment*). This involves attempting to develop common understanding of the purpose of assessment and confronting the extreme view of academic autonomy held by some faculty. *Wading Through Glue* describes a programme- rather than course-based example of faculty working together to develop common understanding and a common instrument.

In *Gain without Pain?* we see an institutional policy that formative assessment should have at least as much emphasis as summative assessment, but in that case and in *Wading Through Glue*, there is explicit comment on the lack of institutional support in the university generally for faculty attempting to develop teaching, learning and assessment.

AUTHENTIC ASSESSMENT AND DEMONSTRATED LEARNING OUTCOMES

'Authentic' assessment refers to the concept that the assessment tasks undertaken by students should have a 'real-life' quality. Examples of movement towards authentic assessment are found in *Assessing Reflection or Supporting Learning?*; *Wading Through Glue*; *The Reflection Jigsaw*; *Portfolios from Cyberia*; *Portfolio Assessment? Yes, but...*; *But They Looked Great on Paper*; and *Making the Grade*.

Demonstrated learning outcomes surface under various guises, especially 'mastery'. The idea here is that students are able to demonstrate that they have attained various important learning outcomes, and this features large in, for example, *IT to the Rescue*, *Gain without Pain?*, *But They Looked Great on Paper* and *Standards + Distance = Trouble?* The prospect of justifying 'value added' through the demonstration of attained learning outcomes should also be mentioned in relation to institutional-level assessment and as described for the entry and exit testing proposed in *Wading Through Glue* or the programme-wide learning outcomes of *Barking at Straw Dogma* and *Towards a Culture of Assessment*.

GENERIC SKILLS AND ABILITIES

Generic skills and abilities are an increasingly important area for the assessment of students and often drive moves towards more authentic assessment vehicles and the demonstration of learning outcomes. Generic skills are tackled in a number of cases. For example, *Assessing Reflection or Supporting Learning?* seeks to develop teamwork, project planning and management; *The Reflection Jigsaw* includes presentation to a panel; and *'Unpacking' Peer Assessment* considers the pros and cons of groupwork, feedback and assessment. Cases that consider the development of generic thinking skills include *But They Looked Great on Paper*, *Read, Think and Be Merry for in Two Weeks Your Assignment Is Due*; and *Refusing to Learn or Learning to Refuse?*, while *Making the Grade* looks at the difficult area of the assessment of interpersonal skills and *Read, Think and Be Merry for in Two Weeks Your Assignment Is Due* also considers cooperative, team-based learning.

FORMATIVE FEEDBACK

The importance of formative feedback is emphasized in a number of the cases. For example, in *IT to the Rescue*, it leads to improved performance and motivation. In this and many other cases (*Gain without Pain?*; *Assessing Reflection or Supporting Learning?*; *'Unpacking' Peer Assessment*; *Ah!… So That's 'Quality'*; *Read, Think and Be Merry for in Two Weeks Your Assignment Is Due*; and *Let's Get the Assessment to Drive the Learning*), there is a conscious blurring of formative and summative assessment. Often, this is a case of students, quite rightly, wanting more feedback on their work while at the same time having their work count summatively. *'Unpacking' Peer Assessment* also raises the issue of providing a balance between negative and positive formative feedback.

Peer and group assessment can also be an excellent vehicle for encouraging formative feedback and developing generic skills and attitudes such as teamwork, reflection and the giving of feedback (*Assessing Reflection or Supporting Learning?*; *'Unpacking' Peer Assessment*; *Ah!… So That's 'Quality'*; *Read, Think and Be Merry for in Two Weeks Your Assignment Is Due*; *Let's Get the Assessment to Drive the Learning*).

CRITERION-REFERENCED ASSESSMENT

There is a clear preference for criterion-referenced assessment in the cases presented in this book. That having been said, there are then significant issues to be resolved concerning such assessment. The need for the criteria to be both clear and clearly understood by all teaching staff and by students is the territory explored in *The Reflection Jigsaw*, *Ah!… So That's 'Quality'* and *Between a Rock and a Hard Place*. Ways of accomplishing this include having the students participate in negotiation and development of criteria (*The Reflection Jigsaw*, *'Unpacking' Peer Assessment*) and the use of exemplars (see below).

VALIDITY, RELIABILITY AND JUDGEMENT

In the introduction, some of the tensions existing between validity (assessing what is intended and what is important) and reliability (assessing consistently) were identified. *Portfolio Assessment? Yes, but…*, *'Unpacking' Peer Assessment*, *Making the Grade*, and *Why Did They Get More than I Did?* are good examples of these tensions being played out in different but equally interesting settings. Of particular concern in these cases is the impact that the number of assessments can have on reliability and validity, and how reliability in the form of staff–staff and staff–student agreement can be developed. It comes as something of a surprise to the case reporters that not only are all assessment judgements not equal, but neither are the teaching practices prior to assessment (see also *Between a Rock and a Hard Place*).

This raises the issue of what we might call 'judgement', which is a central focus for *Ah!... So That's 'Quality'* and *Why Did They Get More than I Did?* Both are fascinating cases that have implications in many areas. The judgement issue concerns whether it is possible to elaborate and weight criteria so explicitly that there is little or no need for further interpretation and professional judgement. How far attempts to minimize judgement could or should go is an interesting point for discussion. Another case where judgement is of importance is *Between a Rock and a Hard Place*.

FLEXIBILITY

Associated with different student profiles and work patterns is the demand for flexibility in assessment (*Gain without Pain?*, *IT to the Rescue*, *Refusing to Learn or Learning to Refuse?*). These cases deal with examples of increasing flexibility in assessment, such as instant access to formative assessment tasks, the opportunity to undertake tasks a number of times, or the possibility of an individual student negotiating the form of the assessment.

Providing a flexible assessment environment also includes teachers demonstrating flexibility when unusual or unexpected situations develop. Intriguing examples of considerable flexibility and 'thinking on one's feet' are seen in many cases, including *Ah!... So That's 'Quality'*, *Let's Get the Assessment to Drive the Learning*, *Refusing to Learn or Learning to Refuse?* and *Organized Chaos*.

EXEMPLARS

The importance of 'exemplars' is noted in *Ah!... So That's 'Quality'*, *Let's Get the Assessment to Drive the Learning*, *Between a Rock and a Hard Place*, *The Reflection Jigsaw*, *Portfolios from Cyberia* and *Standards + Distance = Trouble?*. The issue here is that even though assessment tasks and criteria may be very clearly specified, or even negotiated with students, there is still a significant difference between an abstract statement of a criterion and the reality of its being embodied in a particular assessment artefact. Exemplars can help bridge what might be called the 'expectation gap' between faculty and students with regard to assessment. As is often the case in education, 'showing' can be far more powerful than 'telling'.

TAKING IT PERSONALLY

A number of cases show clearly just how 'personal' assessment tends to be from the perspective of both students and staff. Assessment really matters and so it is no surprise to find the depth of emotion and concern that arises in some of the cases. Good examples of this are found in *Making the Grade, Ah!... So That's 'Quality', Refusing to Learn or Learning to Refuse?* and *Organized Chaos.*

COURAGE

The final area to which we would like to draw attention is the courage of case writers in 'baring' themselves, 'warts and all', for the benefit of others. Assessment has long tended to be a 'closed', individual and autonomous activity. In this it mirrors the whole profession of higher education teaching. The higher education teacher has, for the most part, had little training in how to teach or assess and has not been required to gain a formal professional qualification, join or participate in a professional higher education society, undergo continuing professional development, or even demonstrate teaching competence to any discernable extent. In a closed and non-reflective environment, fully exposing one's practice, including mistakes and misjudgements as well as triumphs, takes considerable courage. However, it is a necessary part of developing as a reflective practitioner, as only by gaining outside comment, critique, interpretation and support can we transcend our present limitations and develop.

We commend the courage of the case reporters in this book and encourage readers to contact them or ourselves to discuss the cases further. We wish you, our readers, every success in transforming and developing your own assessment practices.

FURTHER READING

Airasian, P W (2001) *Classroom Assessment*, McGraw-Hill, New York

Angelo, T A and Cross, K P (1993) *Classroom Assessment Techniques: A handbook for college teachers* (2nd edn), Jossey-Bass, San Francisco, CA

Assessment and Evaluation in Higher Education (journal)

Assessment in Education (journal)

Athanasou, J A (1997) *Introduction to Educational Testing*, Social Science Press, Wentworth Falls, NSW, Australia

Atkins, M J, Beattie, J and Dockrell, W B (1993) *Assessment Issues in Higher Education*, Department of Employment, London

Banta, T W and Associates (1993) *Making a Difference: Outcomes of a decade of assessment in higher education*, Jossey-Bass, San Francisco, CA

Biggs, J B and Collis, K F (1982) *Evaluating the Quality of Learning: The SOLO taxonomy*, Academic Press, New York

Black, P and Wiliam, D (1998) 'Assessment and classroom learning', *Assessment in Education*, **5**, pp 7–74

Black, P and Wiliam, D (1998) 'Inside the black box: raising standards through classroom assessment', *Phi Delta Kappan*, **80**, pp 139–48

Boud, D (1986) *Implementing Student Self-assessment*, Green Guide No. 5, Higher Education Research and Development Society of Australasia, Kensington, NSW, Australia

Boud, D (1995) *Enhancing Learning through Self Assessment*, Kogan Page, London

Brookhart, S M (1999) *The Art and Science of Classroom Assessment: The missing part of pedagogy*, ASHE-ERIC Higher Education Report (Vol. 27, No. 1), The George Washington University, Graduate School of Education and Human Development, Washington, DC

Brown, S, Bull, J and Race, P (1999) *Computer-assisted Assessment in Higher Education*, Kogan Page, London

Brown, S and Glasner, A (eds) (1999) *Assessment Matters in Higher Education: Choosing and using diverse approaches*, Society for Research into Higher Education & Open University Press, Buckingham, UK

Brown, S and Knight, P (1994) *Assessing Learners in Higher Education*, Kogan Page, London

Brown, S, Race, P and Smith, B (1996) *500 Tips on Assessment*, Kogan Page, London

Brown, S and Smith, B (1997) *Getting to Grips with Assessment*, Staff and Educational Development Association, Birmingham, UK

Courts, P L and McInerney, K H (1993) *Assessment in Higher Education: Politics, pedagogy, and portfolios*, Praeger, Westport, CT

Crooks, T J (1988) *Assessing Student Performance*, Green Guide No. 8, Higher Education Research and Development Society of Australasia, Kensington, NSW, Australia

Crooks, T J (1988) 'The impact of classroom evaluation practices on students', *Review of Educational Research*, **58**, pp 438–81

Crooks, T J, Kane, M T and Cohen, A S (1996) 'Threats to the valid use of assessments', *Educational Assessment: Principles, Policy and Practice*, **3**, pp 265–85

Crouch, M K and Fontaine, S I (1994) 'Student portfolios as an assessment tool', in D F Halpern and Associates, *Changing College Classrooms: New teaching and learning strategies for an increasingly complex world*, pp 306–28, Jossey-Bass, San Francisco, CA

Cullingford, C (ed) (1997) *Assessment versus Evaluation*, Cassell, London

Ebel, R L and Frisbie, D A (1991) *Essentials of Educational Measurement* (5th edn), Prentice-Hall, Englewood Cliffs, NJ

Edwards, A and Knight, P (eds) (1995) *Assessing Competence in Higher Education*, Kogan Page, London

Ewell, P, Hutchings, P and Marchese, T (1991) *Reprise 1991: Reprints of two papers treating assessment's history and implementation*, AAHE Assessment Forum, American Association for Higher Education, Washington, DC

Freeman, R and Lewis, R (1998) *Planning and Implementing Assessment*, Kogan Page, London

Gardiner, L F, Anderson, C and Cambridge, B L (eds) (1997) *Learning through Assessment: A resource guide for higher education*, American Association for Higher Education, Washington, DC

George, J and Cowan, J (1999) *A Handbook of Techniques for Formative Evaluation: Mapping the student's learning experience*, Kogan Page, London

Gibbs, G (ed) (1985) *Alternatives in Assessment. 1: Case studies*, Occasional paper no. 18, Standing Conference on Educational Development Services in Polytechnics, Birmingham, UK

Gibbs, G (ed) (1985) *Alternatives in Assessment. 2: Objective tests and computer applications*, Occasional paper no. 21, Standing Conference on Educational Development Services in Polytechnics, Birmingham, UK

Gibbs, G (ed) (no date) *Improving Student Learning Through Assessment and Evaluation*, Oxford Centre for Staff Development, Oxford

Gipps, C V (1994) *Beyond Testing: Towards a theory of educational assessment*, Falmer, London

Gray, P J and Banta, T W (eds) (1997) *The Campus-level Impact of Assessment: Progress, problems, and possibilities*, Jossey-Bass, San Francisco, CA

Gronlund, N E (1988) *How To Construct Achievement Tests* (4th edn), Prentice-Hall, Englewood Cliffs, NJ

Gronlund, N E (1998) *Assessment of Student Achievement* (6th edn), Allyn and Bacon, Boston, MA

Habeshaw, S, Gibbs, G and Habeshaw, T (1993) *53 Interesting Ways to Assess Your Students* (3rd edn), Technical and Educational Services Ltd, Bristol

Heywood, J (2000) *Assessment in Higher Education: Student learning, teaching, programmes and institutions* (rev edn), Jessica Kingsley, London

Hopkins, K D, Stanley, J C and Hopkins, B R (1990) *Educational and Psychological Measurement and Evaluation* (7th edn), Prentice-Hall, Englewood Cliffs, NJ

Huba, M E and Freed, J E (2000) *Learner-centered Assessment on College Campuses: Shifting the focus from teaching to learning*, Allyn and Bacon, Boston, MA

Hutchings, P, Marchese, T and Wright, B (1991) *Using Assessment to Strengthen General Education*, AAHE Assessment Forum, American Association for Higher Education, Washington, DC

Kifer, E (2001) *Large-scale Assessment: Dimensions, dilemmas, and policy*, Corwin Press, Thousand Oaks, CA

Knight, P (ed) (1995) *Assessment for Learning in Higher Education*, Kogan Page, London

Lambert, D and Lines, D (2000) *Monitoring and Assessment*, Falmer, Washington, DC

Linn, R L and Gronlund, N E (1999) *Measurement and Assessment in Teaching* (8th edn), Merrill, Upper Saddle River, NJ

Mager, R F (1997) *Measuring Instructional Results, or, Got a Match?: How to find out if your instructional objectives have been achieved* (3rd edn), Center for Effective Performance, Atlanta, GA

McMillan, J H (ed) (1988) *Assessing Students' Learning*, New Directions for Teaching and Learning, no. 34, Jossey-Bass, San Francisco, CA

Miller, A H, Imrie, B W and Cox, K (1998) *Student Assessment in Higher Education: A handbook for assessing performance*, Kogan Page, London

Milton, O (1982) *Will That Be on the Final?!*, Charles C Thomas, Springfield, IL

Nightingale, P, Te Wiata, I, Toohey, S, Ryan, G, Hughes, C and Magin, D (1996) *Assessing Learning in Universities*, University of New South Wales Press, Sydney

Nitko, A J (2001) *Educational Assessment of Students* (3rd edn), Merrill, Upper Saddle River, NJ

Nummedal, S G (1994) 'How classroom assessment can improve teaching and learning', in D F Halpern and Associates, *Changing College Classrooms: New teaching and learning strategies for an increasingly complex world*, pp 289–305, Jossey-Bass, San Francisco, CA

Nuttall, D L (1986) *Assessing Educational Achievement*, Falmer Press, London

Palomba, C A and Banta, T W (1999) *Assessment Essentials: Planning, implementing, and improving assessment in higher education*, Jossey-Bass, San Francisco, CA

Payne, D A (1992) *Measuring and Evaluating Educational Outcomes*, Merrill, New York

Phye G D (1996) *Handbook of Classroom Assessment*, Academic Press, New York

Popham, W J (1993) *Educational Evaluation* (3rd edn), Allyn and Bacon, Boston, MA

Race, P (1993) *Never Mind the Teaching, Feel the Learning*, Staff and Educational Development Association, Birmingham, UK

Ratcliff, J L (1994) 'Assessment's role in strengthening the core curriculum', in D F Halpern and Associates, *Changing College Classrooms: New teaching and learning strategies for an increasingly complex world*, pp 329–48, Jossey-Bass, San Francisco, CA

Rowntree, D (1987) *Assessing Students: How shall we know them?* (rev edn), Kogan Page, London

Sadler, D R (1989) 'Formative assessment and the design of instructional systems', *Instructional Science*, **18**, pp 191–209

Thorndike, R M (1997) *Measurement and Evaluation in Psychology and Education* (6th edn), Merrill, Upper Saddle River, NJ

Weber, E (1999) *Student Assessment that Works: A practical approach*, Allyn and Bacon, Boston, MA

Weedon, P, Winter, J and Broadfoot, P (2001) *Assessment*, Routledge Falmer, London

Wolff, R A and Harris, O D (1994) 'Using assessment to develop a culture of evidence', in D F Halpern and Associates, *Changing College Classrooms: New teaching and learning strategies for an increasingly complex world*, pp 271–88, Jossey-Bass, San Francisco, CA

Index